WILMORTON

Practical Approaches to Literary Criticism

general editor
Richard Adams

Poems

Philip Robinson

Longman

Longman Group UK Limited,
Longman House, Burnt Mill, Harlow,
Essex CM20 2JE, England
and Associated Companies throughout the world.

First published 1988

Set in 10/12 point Linotron 202 Baskerville

Produced by Longman Group (FE) Ltd
Printed in Hong Kong

ISBN 0 582 35531 1

6　Poems to compare 89

Introduction

If you have followed one of the GCSE courses available in English, you will already have some experience of using poetry as a stimulus for your own creative writing and of developing some critical judgement in your reading of it. The aim of this book is to give you further experience in the second of these approaches to poetry and to provide you with some of the apparatus you need if you are to discuss and write about poetry with confidence. In the course of looking at the poems in this book, opportunities will arise for introducing some technical terms. Some of these may be familiar, others new, but all are presented simply as a help in appreciating the skill of the poet. Poetry is there to be read and enjoyed; as far as this book is concerned, 'studying' poetry consists of looking more closely at the techniques by which poets achieve their effects, as an aid to greater understanding and pleasure.

Either before or after each poem, or pair of poems, you will find a number of questions. They are intended to give some sense of direction when you start to think about what you read, but how you use them is up to you. You may wish to discuss or write about each individual question, or you may prefer to see them as guides to the issues you should discuss in a longer piece of writing. In either case, they are intended as guidelines, not as comprehension exercises.

Two final points. If you are to enjoy poetry to the full, you must get into the habit of reading it out aloud. First and foremost, poetry communicates to the ear; it has its roots in what is called 'oral tradition', our habit of turning our experiences into verse which can be repeated, elaborated and remembered. The great virtue of rhyme, so often used in English poetry, is that it makes verse memorable. Of course, you may not always have the opportunity to read out aloud; it is essentially a private activity and not easily practised in public places! Second best is to learn to read aloud in your

Contents

4   Variety of approach: animals   56

5   The personal touch   72

head. This is not a very useful technique if you have a lengthy textbook to work through, but a poem gains immensely from being read in a way that allows you to 'hear' it as well as see it on the page. You will find that your enjoyment of it increases very considerably – as well as your understanding.

This book is not intended to be a comprehensive introduction to poets writing in English; such a major figure as Milton, for example, makes no appearance at all. None the less I have tried to introduce quite a wide variety of poets and I hope that amongst them you will find individuals whose work you are encouraged to pursue through your wider reading. A great deal of stimulation and pleasure awaits you if you do.

1 Starting points

How do poems start? By that I mean: what is it that causes a writer to create a particular poem? The answer is inevitably diverse, but in this opening chapter I want to begin by looking at one possible source of an idea for a poem: a visual *image*. In both the poems which follow the writer has taken as a jumping-off point a simple action: the wave of a hand.

Not Waving but Drowning

Nobody heard him, the dead man,
But still he lay moaning:
I was much further out than you thought
And not waving but drowning.

5   Poor chap, he always loved larking
And now he's dead
It must have been too cold for him his heart gave way,
They said.

10   Oh, no no no, it was too cold always
(Still the dead one lay moaning)
I was much too far out all my life
And not waving but drowning.

Stevie Smith

The heart of this poem is the contrast between the two possible interpretations of the man's wave. To observers on the shore his gesture was a happy one; he seemed to be enjoying himself in the water and was waving to communicate his enjoyment.

1

The truth was very different: in trouble, he was desperately seeking to draw their attention to his plight – he was not waving but drowning. Alas, they found this out too late to be of any help to him.

As a literal description of a tragic accident this would be poignant enough; you can imagine the impact that this account might make in the hands of a gifted journalist, writing in a popular newspaper. But poetry can go beyond reporting, and a second reading of the poem reveals that the simple image of the waving man has been developed to suggest a wider meaning. The first two verses present the incident mainly from the view of the onlookers, but in the third the poet does what a reporter could not: she makes the dead man himself speak out, to show to them a further misunderstanding. He was too far out *all his life*. As readers we are left to consider this statement. Clearly we are looking here at more than a swimming accident; the dead man tells us that throughout his life he was in difficulties, but it is only after his death that those who could have helped him realise his need. With that idea in mind, we can look again at a remark earlier in the poem: 'Poor chap, he always loved larking' (line 5). Was the cheerful face he presented to the world the emotional equivalent of the wave of the drowning man? Was he trying to summon help? We are left to guess why his life was unhappy, why it was 'too cold always'. The poem is not a case history. None the less, it steps beyond the facts and into the world of the imagination.

In the poem by Thomas Hardy which follows, a similar pattern appears: a visual image starts a train of thought which is at first developed in simple style. Again the image is of a waving hand, this time the hand of a woman whose husband has been defeated in an election. She stands on the balcony, facing the crowd who by opposing him have 'doomed her lord's cause'. They are turbulent and loud, like the 'surging sea', but she seeks to put a brave face on her disappointment, 'Smiling, while hurt'.

The Rejected Member's Wife

We shall see her no more
    On the balcony,
Smiling, while hurt, at the roar
    As of surging sea
5 From the stormy sturdy band
    Who have doomed her lord's cause,
Though she waves her little hand
    As it were applause.

Here will be candidates yet,
10   And candidates' wives.
Fervid with zeal to set
    Their ideals on our lives:
Here will come market-men
    On the market-days,
15 Here will clash now and then
    More such party assays.

And the balcony will fill
    When such times are renewed,
And the throng in the street will thrill
20   With today's mettled mood;
But she will no more stand
    In the sunshine there,
With that wave of her white-gloved hand,
    And that chestnut hair.

Thomas Hardy

Unlike Stevie Smith's poem, this one does not allow the waving figure to speak; we view her entirely through the eyes of the poet. None the less Hardy does rather more than paint the picture; he includes in the middle part of the poem some of his own wry reflections about politics, in his suggestion that campaigners are 'fervid with zeal to set/Their ideals on our lives' (lines 11–12). In the end, however, we return to the image, to the contrast between the excited and assertive crowd in the street and the vulnerable, delicate woman who stands, chestnut hair glowing in the sunshine, waving her white-gloved hand.

Both these poems involve a personal reaction to a visual stimulus. Consider the following.

- Which poet creates more clearly the picture of what has occurred?
- Which one makes you feel more strongly the emotions involved?
- In Stevie Smith's poem, what is the effect of making the dead man speak?
- What impression of the poet himself do you gain from reading Thomas Hardy's poem?

Hardy was a poet to whom such pictures were very important; he had a gift for storing them away in his memory for many years and then realising them vividly in his poems long afterwards. But for many poets the spring-board of a poem is a stimulus to the senses of one kind or another: visual as in the two poems we have just looked at, or in case of the next poem, one of taste.

The title tells us what this poem is: an imitation of the sort of note that you might find left on the kitchen table, when you come into the room expecting someone to be there. In this case, the note is a sort of excuse, though not a very satisfactory one: 'the plums were there so I ate them'. The additional information that they were delicious adds insult to injury. The poem centres on their taste: 'so sweet and so cold'. In the last four lines we can savour this cold, delicious sweetness. It seems to me to be impossible to read this poem without tasting the plums in your mouth. A short poem such as this communicates very directly, but it also encourages the imagination to supply what it leaves out. In Stevie Smith's poem we know a little about the dead man and can guess some more, but here we are given almost nothing and so speculation can run riot. To whom is the note addressed? Why was it left just before breakfast? Before long, you can end up with the picture of a lover creeping out of the house before the girl he is leaving behind wakes (or with the sexes reversed, of course!). Suddenly the note takes on poignancy; the reckless yielding to irresistible temptation, so inadequately excused, might stand for more than just gulping down a few plums. The departing guest might well have taken advantage of more than just the contents of the refrigerator. Far-fetched, perhaps? Yet the poem gives greater freedom to the imagination than any factual account would allow.

This is Just to Say

I have eaten
the plums
that were in
the icebox

5   and which
you were probably
saving
for breakfast

Forgive me
10 they were delicious
so sweet
and so cold

William Carlos Williams

• Does there seem to you to be any particular point in the way the poem is laid out? Would anything have been lost had all twelve lines been run together?

The next two poems are about autumn. The first has the simplicity of the previous poem.

Autumn

A touch of cold in the Autumn night –
I walked abroad,
And saw the ruddy moon lean over a hedge
Like a red-faced farmer.
5   I did not stop to speak, but nodded,
And round about were the wistful stars
With white faces like town children.

T E Hulme

- What images are the stimulus for this poem?
- Does it offer anything more than simple description?

The second poem has a similar title, but approaches the subject of autumn in a much fuller way.

To Autumn

I

Season of mists and mellow fruitfulness,
   Close bosom friend of the maturing sun,
Conspiring with him how to load and bless
   With fruit the vines that round the thatch-eves run:
5   To bend with apples the mossed cottage-trees,
     And fill all fruit with ripeness to the core;
      To swell the gourd, and plump the hazel shells
     With a sweet kernel; to set budding more,
   And still more, later flowers for the bees,
10 Until they think warm days will never cease,
     For summer has o'er-brimmed their clammy cells.

II

Who hath not seen thee oft amid thy store?
    Sometimes whoever seeks abroad may find
Thee sitting careless on a granary floor,
15   Thy hair soft-lifted by the winnowing wind;
Or on a half-reaped furrow sound asleep,
    Drowsed with the fume of poppies, while thy hook
      Spares the next swath and all its twinèd flowers;
And sometimes like a gleaner thou dost keep
20   Steady thy laden head across a brook;
    Or by a cyder-press, with patient look,
      Thou watches the last oozings hours by hours.

III

Where are the songs of spring? Aye, where are they?
    Think not of them, thou hast thy music too —
25 While barrèd clouds bloom the soft-dying day,
    And touch the stubble-plains with rosy hue.
Then in a wailful choir the small gnats mourn
    Among the river sallows, borne aloft
      Or sinking as the light wind lives or dies;
30   And full-grown lambs loud bleat from hilly bourn;
    Hedge-crickets sing; and now with treble soft
    The red-breast whistles from a garden-croft;
      And gathering swallows twitter in the skies.

John Keats

This poem may well present some initial difficulties. To begin
with, it was written in the early nineteenth century, and some
of the activity it describes may seem unfamiliar. Few people
these days spend their time crushing apples in a cider press;
the harvest tasks of reaping, gleaning and winnowing would
now be performed by machines. Recourse to a dictionary
might be needed to explain these terms, and also some unusual
words: 'gourd' (line 7), 'sallows' (line 28), 'bourn' (line 30).

When you have clear in your mind the details in the poem, then approach it once more from the point of view of stimulus.

- What are the dominant visual images in this poem?
- To what extent does the poet arouse other senses: hearing? touch?
- What is the effect of dividing the poem into three verses? Are there links between the images presented in each verse which help to make the verses coherent?

- The richness of the language in this poem distinguishes it from any other we have encountered yet in this section. Examine some of these effects. Look, for instance, at the four verbs which dominate lines 5–8: 'bend', 'fill', 'swell', 'plump'. What do they suggest about the nature of autumn?

This poem also makes effective use of a popular literary device: *personification*. Throughout this poem, Keats addresses the season of autumn as if it were a person. For example, it is pictured as being a 'Close bosom friend of the maturing sun,/ Conspiring with him'. This device allows writers to give a sense of physical reality to abstract things. In the next chapter (page 24) we will see John Donne treating death as a figure which can be spoken to.

- Consider personification in the second verse of the poem? How does Keats use it to develop our picture of the nature of autumn?

The poem also raises another question of great interest to literary critics: how much does it enhance our understanding of a poem to know something of the life of its author? Should a text speak wholly for itself? Do we risk misinterpreting it if we allow our reading of it to be affected by our knowledge of matters external to it? Take, for example, the poem earlier in this chapter in which Hardy describes the wife of a defeated electoral candidate (page 3). We know that this poem was published in 1906, the year of a general election. An enthusiastic biographer would be able to tell us of a constituency visited by Hardy at election time; he could even put a name to the 'rejected member' and tell us something of his background. Would this be of importance to us in terms of our understanding and appreciation of the poem? I doubt it. The picture Hardy paints needs no explanation; it is poignant in itself. The information might be interesting from a biographical point of view, but is irrelevant to our response to the poem; it might even get in the way.

This argument is relevant to Keats's 'To Autumn'. We can date this poem almost exactly to Sunday, 19 September 1819. We know from a letter written two days later that an afternoon walk inspired him to describe with such delight the qualities of autumn celebrated in the first two verses. A wider view of Keats's life would remind us that already by that September his health was suffering under the onslaught of the tuberculosis which would kill him in less than a year and a half. His brother Tom had died in December of the previous year of the same condition; Keats had watched his slow and painful decline. The onset of winter had sealed his brother's fate. In 1820 Keats tried to escape the same harsh effects of climate by fleeing to milder Italy; yet he died there in February 1821. You could argue therefore that to Keats autumn has a special significance: it is a season of great beauty, but it also heralds winter, with its associations of suffering and death. The joys of autumn can be seen as all too fragile.

- Consider the last verse in the light of this idea. What is its atmosphere and how do the images described contribute to it?
- Does a knowledge of some details of Keats's life have any effect on your reaction to the ending of the poem?

The two final poems in this chapter take as their starting point a fatal accident: Philip Larkin's 'The Explosion' is concerned

with a mining disaster; Robert Frost's poem 'Out, Out – '
describes a boy who cuts off his hand in an accident.

● Look first at the description of the build-up to the accident.
  What is its *tone*? If you were to read the piece aloud, what
  expression would you put into your voice: harsh and bitter?
  soft and gentle? angry? calm?

● How does Frost bring out the reactions of the boy to what
  happens to him?

● How does he use personification (see page 8) here?

Out, Out –

The buzz saw snarled and rattled in the yard
And made dust and dropped stove-length sticks of
  wood.
Sweet-scented stuff when the breeze drew across it.
And from there those that lifted eyes could count
5 Five mountain ranges one behind the other
Under the sunset far into Vermont.
And the saw snarled and rattled, snarled and
  rattled,
As it ran light, or had to bear a load.
And nothing happened: day was all but done.
10 Call it a day, I wish they might have said
To please the boy by giving him the half hour
That a boy counts so much when saved from work.
His sister stood beside them in her apron
To tell them 'Supper'. At the word, the saw,
15 As if to prove saws knew what supper meant,
Leaped out at the boy's hand, or seemed to leap –
He must have given the hand. However it was,
Neither refused the meeting. But the hand!
The boy's first outcry was a rueful laugh,
20 As he swung toward them holding up the hand
Half in appeal, but half as if to keep

The life from spilling. Then the boy saw all —
Since he was old enough to know, big boy
Doing a man's work, though a child at heart —
25 He saw all spoiled. 'Don't let him cut my hand off —
The doctor, when he comes. Don't let him sister!'
So. But the hand was gone already.
The doctor put him in the dark of ether.
He lay and puffed his lips out with his breath.
30 And then — the watcher at his pulse took fright.
No one believed. They listened at his heart.
Little — less — nothing! — and that ended it.
No more to build on there. And they, since they
Were not the one dead, turned to their affairs.

Robert Frost

The title contains a literary reference you may well recognise. Near the end of Shakespeare's *Macbeth*, the tyrant Macbeth hears of the death of his wife. In a famous speech, he expresses his sense of the futility, the pointlessness of life:

Out, out, brief candle!
Life's but a walking shadow, a poor player,
That struts and frets his hour upon the stage,
And then is heard no more: it is a tale
Told by an idiot, full of sound and fury,
Signifying nothing.
Act V, sc. 5, lines 23–28

Shakespeare uses a vivid image here to suggest the impermanence of life: an actor who plays his brief part and then disappears for ever. He also compares life to a candle which can be abruptly snuffed out.

● How does the title help you to understand the last few lines of the poem?

The Explosion

On the day of the explosion
Shadows pointed towards the pithead:
In the sun the slagheap slept.

Down the lane came men in pitboots
5   Coughing oath-edged talk and pipe-smoke,
Shouldering off the freshened silence.

One chased after rabbits; lost them;
Came back with a nest of lark's eggs;
Showed them; lodged them in the grasses.

10 So they passed in beards and moleskins,
Fathers, brothers, nicknames, laughter,
Through the tall gates standing open.

At noon, there came a tremor; cows
Stopped chewing for a second; sun,
15 Scarfed as in a heat-haze, dimmed.

The dead go on before us, they
Are sitting in God's house in comfort,
We shall see them face to face —

Plain as lettering in the chapels
20 It was said, and for a second
Wives saw men of the explosion

Larger than in life they managed —
Gold as on a coin, or walking
Somehow from the sun towards them,

25 One showing the eggs unbroken.

Philip Larkin

As in Frost's poem, the subject here is a fatal accident, this time in a coal mine. The treatment is very different.

- Look at the first four verses. What kind of atmosphere do they create? What impression do we receive of these miners?
- Look at some of the phrases Larkin uses. The miners are 'shouldering off the freshened silence'. What picture of them does this create? How can you shoulder off silence?
- Look at the last line of the fourth verse. Is there particular significance in Larkin's description of the miners as walking 'through the tall gates standing open'?
- Now look at the rest of the poem. Why is the sixth verse written in italics?
- What does the vision which the wives see 'for a second' (line 20) tell us about their feelings? Why do the men appear 'Larger than in life' (line 22)?
- Finally, consider the impact of the final line. Why does Larkin set it apart from the rest of the poem? Why does he consider this detail to have been significant enough to use as the ending of the poem?

A poem like Larkin's 'The Explosion' gives us the opportunity to make some tentative steps towards a discussion of *metre*. First, a dictionary definition: 'Metre in poetry is the recurring pattern of stressed and unstressed syllables.' All words are made up of syllables, separate vowel sounds to which groups of consonants can be attached. So 'life' has one syllable, 'lar-ger' two, 'let-ter-ing' three, and so on. When we speak these words, we *stress* some syllables more strongly than others. 'Monday', for example, we say with the stress on the first syllable; in 'today' on the other hand, we stress the second. Sometimes we need stress to tell us what word we are using. Stress 'desert' on the second syllable, for example, and you have a verb meaning abandon; stress it on the first and you have a noun meaning an area of barren land. In poetry, these stresses of syllables can be repeated to form patterns. In the case of 'The

Explosion', for instance, reading the poem aloud brings out the characteristics of its metre. We realise that the tendency is to stress alternate syllables in a pattern of: stress; unstress; stress; unstress:

> *Down* the *lane* came *men* in *pit*boots
> *Cough*ing *oath*-edged *talk* and *pipe*-smoke
>   (lines 4–5).

This singsong rhythm is known as *trochaic* and was most famously used by Henry Longfellow in his poem 'The song of Hiawatha'. For example,

> By the shores of Gitche Gumee,
> By the shining Big-Sea-Water,
> Stood the wigwam of Nokomis,
> Daughter of the Moon, Nokomis.
> 5 Dark behind it rose the forest,
> Rose the black and gloomy pine-trees,
> Rose the firs with cones upon them;

If you read this extract out loud, you will quickly find yourself falling into its distinctive rhythm. Larkin uses this pattern of stresses for almost all the verses of 'The Explosion'. But there are exceptions.

- In which parts of the poem does Larkin choose not to use this trochaic metre? Can you see any reason for his choice?

Many English words have a trochaic rhythm – for instance, ones that end in -ing like 'talking' or 'sleeping' or in -ed like 'landed' or 'wounded' – but very little English poetry has used a regular trochaic pattern for its metre. However, the opposite of trochaic, known as *iambic*, has had an immense influence. Iambics have the pattern: unstress; stress; unstress; stress. Most verbs with two syllables are iambic: 'delay'; 'desire;

'depart'. Shakespeare's plays make extensive use of iambic metre – not all the time of course, because that would lead to monotony. If you look at, say, the opening Chorus of *Romeo and Juliet*, you will see how the iambic rhythm dominates:

CHORUS

Two households, both alike in dignity,
   In fair Verona where we lay our scene,
From ancient grudge break to new mutiny,
   Where civil blood makes civil hands unclean.
5 From forth the fatal loins of these two foes
   A pair of star-cross'd lovers take their life;
Whose misadventur'd, piteous overthrows
   Doth with their death bury their parents' strife.

If you read these lines aloud, you will see how the stress tends to fall on alternate syllables: 'From *forth* the *fat*al *loins* of *these* two *foes*'. You can, of course, introduce variations as you read; you might well want to put some stress on the word 'two' in that line, as well as 'foes'. Metre is not meant to be a strait-jacket into which poetry is forced. But the above lines show a distinct tendency towards an iambic pattern of stress. Actors speaking the lines may choose to underline certain words for their own particular reasons, but if they resist the metre too ruthlessly, the flow of the poetry must suffer.

Looking at poetry in this way, observing the way it is put together, can greatly increase your enjoyment of it, as you begin to appreciate the skill of the poet. Some readers of poetry are content simply to respond to the poem on the page and do not wish to look further. Such a standpoint is of course perfectly valid. Others, however, enjoy the consideration of how a poet achieves his effects. This does not mean that they cease to enjoy the poem as an entity in itself. Those who are at first reluctant to 'study' poetry often use the analogy of pulling a flower to pieces to see how it is made. 'When you have finished', they say, 'all that is left is a heap of torn petals.

The beauty of the flower is destroyed for ever.' They may be right about flowers, but the work of a gifted poet is a very durable commodity: you can break it down into its constituent parts, you can write great volumes on Shakespeare's use of the semi-colon, if you are so inclined, but the poetry can remain just as fresh and unbruised as when you read it for the first time.

In the next chapter, we will continue the discussion about how poetry is put together by looking particularly at the question of *form*. To focus our attention, we will concentrate on just one well-known kind of poem, the sonnet.

2 Form and ideas: the sonnet

The sonnet is essentially an Italian form, originating in the thirteenth century and brought to a high degree of sophistication by great masters such as Petrarch and Dante. It made its appearance in England in about 1527, when Sir Thomas Wyatt, a diplomat in the court of King Henry VIII, visited Italy and became fascinated by the splendour of the poetry he found there. The sonnet is a very restricted form -- to qualify as a sonnet, a poem must have exactly fourteen lines – yet it has proved a popular one from the moment of its introduction to the present day. It is a form which can allow the writer to balance style and content in a stimulating way. In this chapter, we look at the two types of sonnet most often used in English poetry, and develop, from our consideration, some thoughts about the relationship between what a poem has to say and the form in which it says it.

Before we think about the ideas contained in the first poem, let us look first at its *shape*. In the introduction I talked about the need to hear a poem as you read it, because all poetry, whether it is dramatic or not, implies a speaking voice. We must not forget, however, that a poem is an object as well as a series of spoken words: it is formed by writing or printing on paper. The shape of that object, the poem, is of interest because the pattern in which the words are arranged affects the way that the ideas come across to the reader. Now, in order to write intelligibly about the shape of a poem, you need to have at your disposal a certain number of critical terms which you can use to describe it. There is of course a danger that too specialised a vocabulary will prevent the reader from grasping the point you are making, or that in your eagerness to highlight certain technical effects you will lose sight of what the poem has to say. Moderation must therefore be the keynote.

On First Looking into Chapman's Homer

Much have I travelled in the realms of gold,
   And many goodly states and kingdoms seen;
   Round many western islands have I been
Which bards in fealty to Apollo hold.
5 Oft of one wide expanse had I been told
   That deep-browed Homer ruled as his demesne;
   Yet did I never breathe its pure serene
Till I heard Chapman speak out loud and bold.
Then felt I like some watcher of the skies
10   When a new planet swims into his ken;
Or like stout Cortez when with eagle eyes
   He stared at the Pacific, and all his men
Looked at each other with a wild surmise –
   Silent, upon a peak in Darien.

John Keats

Keats's poem largely follows the pattern known as the Petrarchan or Italian sonnet. That is to say, it is divided into two groups of lines: a group of eight, known as the *octave*, and a group of six, known as the *sestet*. Usually this division has a significant effect on the way the ideas are developed in the poem; the octave often contains the statement and elaboration of a theme, whereas the sestet introduces a change of direction, a new way of looking at the subject. This change is known as the turn, or *volta*. The Italian origin of this kind of poetry reveals itself in the vocabulary used to describe it. Keats's sonnet has this basic shape. His octave consists of two sets of four lines; in each set the first and fourth lines rhyme, as do the second and third. Writing about rhyme can present difficulties, and to avoid clumsiness a simple device of lettering can be used. The last word of each line is given a letter: thus 'gold' is A and 'seen' is B. If the last word of any of the succeeding lines rhymes with that of a previous one, it is given the same letter: thus 'hold' in line 4, rhyming with 'gold' in line 1, is also given the letter A. When this process is completed, you have a series of letters representing the pattern of rhymes in the poem. Thus the *rhyme scheme* for Keats's octave reads 'ABBA ABBA'. Once you get over the unfamiliarity and apparent artificiality of this system, you will see that it is in fact a much easier way of pointing out how rhyme works in a poem than going through the business of expressing it in words. The scheme of the sestet could be described as employing alternately rhyming lines using the same two rhymes throughout; 'CD CD CD' seems a clearer and less clumsy way of describing what is happening.

But what about the meaning of the poem itself? Poems are more than just arrangements of lines and rhymes. 'On First Looking into Chapman's Homer' presents us with the initial difficulty of its peculiar title. Recourse to a work of reference such as the *Oxford Companion to English Literature* clears up the problem: Chapman was George Chapman, a poet and drama-tist who wrote in the early seventeenth century, and his 'Homer' was his translation of the epic poems of the ancient Greek poet Homer: *The Iliad* and *The Odyssey*. Keats's 'first looking into' it – that is to say, his first reading of it – created the experience described in the poem. The octave reveals the extent of his previous reading of classical poetry, expressed in terms of a journey through 'realms of gold'. The experience is dressed up in what sounds like archaic language: poets are described as 'bards in fealty to Apollo' and a home is a 'demesne'. This is what is often called *poetic diction* – language of a dignified and ornate kind such as might be considered suitable for the expression of lofty ideas or scenes of beauty.

In the sestet Keats changes the direction of the poem to describe the impact of reading Chapman's translation for the first time. He does it through the use of two images: sighting a new planet and discovering a new ocean. The turn, or *volta*, is emphasised by a change of language. If you look at the last six lines of the poem, you will see that they are much simpler and clearer in terms of vocabulary; 'all his men/Looked at each other' is very much everyday language. The experience of reading Chapman is quite different from anything that has gone before. The great strength of the poem is undoubtedly the power of the visual image it creates: the explorer and his men suddenly faced with a vast expanse of inexplicable ocean; their expressions of astonishment as they struggle to come to terms with the extraordinary realisation that what they are standing on must be a new and previously undiscovered continent, that it cannot after all be Asia as they had thought. This image would be a powerful one however it was presented, but the way the shape of the poem brings it into the flow of ideas gives it particular emphasis. The poem moves from the past to the present, from the flowery to the simple, from the general to the specific, from the octave to the sestet. Form and meaning go hand in hand.

The Italian form of the sonnet is the original, but not the most common. More often seen in English is the form named after Shakespeare, its greatest exponent.

It does not take long to see that we are dealing with a different kind of sonnet here (page 21). Attempts to split it into two blocks of eight and six, the octave and the sestet, founder on the rhyme scheme of the poem. It clearly divides itself into three groups of four lines. Their rhyme scheme is ABAB CDCD EFEF, and the poem ends with two lines rhyming successively, which is called a *rhyming couplet*. The turn, the change of direction after eight lines, which is a feature of Italian sonnets, cannot work here. The way that the poem is arranged means that the three blocks of four lines form a very different pattern from the one we saw in Keats's poem.

That time of year thou mayst in me behold

That time of year thou mayst in me behold
  When yellow leaves, or none, or few, do hang
Upon those boughs which shake against the cold,
  Bare ruined choirs, where late the sweet birds
     sang.
5 In me thou seest the twilight of such day
  As after sunset fadeth in the west;
Which by and by black night doth take away,
  Death's second self, that seals up all in rest.
In me thou seest the glowing of such fire,
10   That on the ashes of his youth doth lie,
As the death-bed whereon it must expire,
  Consumed with that which it was nourished by.
    This thou perceiv'st, which makes thy love more
     strong,
15   To love that well which thou must leave ere long.

William Shakespeare

The content of the poem is naturally shaped by its form. We see that Shakespeare has used the three units of four lines each to present three images which are both separate and inter-linked. The first four describe autumn, the time of year when 'yellow leaves' hang on the bare branches and the cold wind shakes the boughs. In the second he describes twilight, the prelude to night, and in the third the ashes of a dying fire. The four lines are made to hold together not just by the rhyme scheme but also by the sentence structure: full stops appear only at the end of each block of four, to reinforce the impression of the completion of one topic before the introduction of the next. Yet all three pictures are linked; they are all stages of transition between one state and another: summer and winter, day and night, a burning fire and dead one. The passage of time is constantly referred to in this poem: 'where

21

late the sweet birds sang' (line 4); 'sunset fadeth in the west' (line 6); 'by and by black night doth take away' (line 7). After these three images are established, Shakespeare still has two more lines at his disposal, and he uses them to reveal the point of the poem. In the final rhyming couplet, he focuses the poem on the person to whom it is addressed: his lover: 'Time is short; death is not far off. Love me now; I shall soon be gone for ever.' The last two lines allow for a 'twist in the tail', the kind of 'turn' in the direction of the poem which the Italian sonnets generally feature at the ninth line rather than the thirteenth. Again we see that the form of the poem is once more tightly linked to the shape of the ideas it carries.

Not all sonnets follow exactly one of these two patterns, but most tend towards one or the other. Consider, for example, this sonnet by Michael Drayton, who wrote at about the the same time as Shakespeare.

Since there's no help, come, let us kiss and part

Since there's no help, come, let us kiss and part –
Nay, I have done: you get no more of me;
And I am glad, yea, glad with all my heart
That thus so cleanly I myself can free.
5 Shake hands forever, cancel all our vows,
And when we meet at any time again,
Be it not seen in either of our brows
That we one jot of former love retain.
Now at the last gasp of love's latest breath,
10 When, his pulse failing, Passion speechless lies,
When Faith is kneeling by his bed of death,
And Innocence is closing up his eyes, –
    Now, if thou wouldst, when all have given him over,
    From death to life thou mightst him yet recover.

Michael Drayton

A glance shows that the rhyme scheme here is the same as that of Shakespeare's sonnet: ABAB CDCD EFEF GG. When we read the poem, however, we find that there is a marked difference. At first, it seems to use the same approach. The opening four lines centre on an action: a kiss. This is not a kiss of passion but of parting; it represents the end of an affair: 'Nay, I have done: you get no more of me'(line 2). As in Shakespeare's sonnet, the lines run through to a full stop at the end of the block of four. (This seems a good point to introduce another technical term, the *quatrain*, to replace the ponderous phrase 'block of four lines'.) The second quatrain follows the pattern of the first: we have another action, this time the shaking of hands, which is again shown to be one of parting; it is 'forever'. Once again the four lines compose one complete sentence. With the pattern of Shakespeare's sonnet in mind, we might expect the next quatrain to introduce another variation on the same theme of a parting gesture – a wave of the hand perhaps? But instead . . .

- Look at the last six lines. How do they differ from our expectations? Their rhyme scheme is standard, but what about the ideas contained within them? And the *volta*, the 'twist in the tail', does that appear solely in the final couplet, or is it prepared for beforehand?

You may well conclude that Drayton has written a sonnet which uses the English form, but takes something from the Italian tradition as well. He uses the rhyme scheme to give the poem one shape – three fours and a two – then arranges the ideas within the framework to suggest another, an eight and a six. Is he doing this just to amuse himself, to show off, even? Not that there is anything particularly wrong in being clever in the use of form. None the less, we may well feel that his purpose is to achieve the best of both worlds: to start off with a shape that allows him two variations on a theme of parting, but then to shift into a form which suggests that even at this late stage the pattern is not inevitable: though love is dying fast, it can still be revived.

● Compare for a moment the last two sonnets, Shakespeare's and Drayton's. Both could be said to be 'love poems'; both seek to persuade a lover. Which do you find the more appealing, the more convincing? How do you account for your preference?

Another example of the freer treatment of the traditional forms of the sonnet is John Donne's poem 'Death, be not proud'.

Death, be not proud

Death, be not proud, though some have callèd thee
    Mighty and dreadful, for thou art not so;
    For those whom thou think'st thou overthrow
Die not, poor Death, nor yet canst thou kill me.
5 From rest and sleep, which but thy pictures be,
    Much pleasure – then, from thee much more must
      flow;
    And soonest our best men with thee do go,
Rest of their bones and soul's delivery.
10 Thou'rt slave to fate, chance, kings and desperate
    men,
    And dost with poison, war, and sickness dwell;
    And poppy or charms can make us sleep as well,
And better than thy stroke. Why swell'st thou then?
15   One short sleep past, we wake eternally,
    And death shall be no more. Death, thou shalt
      die.

                            John Donne

Donne wrote a number of these 'Holy Sonnets' in the early part of the seventeenth century. They are almost all characterised by the tone of passionate argument which can be seen here. A glance at the line-endings of the poem shows the rhyme scheme to be ABBA ABBA CDDC EE. This is clearly a mixture of the English and the Italian. The scheme of the first eight lines leads you to expect a similar shape of poem to that of Keats's sonnet previously quoted (see page 18). This is the Italian form, and would normally be followed by the sestet, the group of six lines arranged in a pattern such as CDE CDE or CD CD CD. Donne, however, breaks away from the expected by using the same rhyme scheme for the next four lines and then ending the poem with a couplet, as an English sonnet would do. So we have a hybrid, a cross between English and Italian. But why does Donne do this?

- Look at the ideas which the poem expresses. How do they fit in with the shape which Donne has given to the poem? What does he gain by twisting the form around in the later stages of the poem?
- Look at the last two lines. The Italian form Donne began with would not normally produce a rhyming couplet. Why did he want one here?

On page 26 is a sonnet written nearly two hundred years later than Donne's.

- Look first at the rhyme scheme. A glance confirms that more than a glance will be needed. See what you make of it.

Ozymandias

I met a traveller from an antique land
Who said: Two vast and trunkless legs of stone
Stand in the desert . . . Near them, on the sand,
Half sunk, a shattered visage lies, whose frown,
5 And wrinkled lip, and sneer of cold command,
Tell that its sculptor well those passions read
Which yet survive, stamped on these lifeless things,
The hand that mocked them, and the heart that fed:
And on the pedestal these words appear:
10 'My name is Ozymandias, king of kings:
Look on my works, ye Mighty, and despair!'
Nothing beside remains. Round the decay
Of that colossal wreck, boundless and bare
The lone and level sands stretch far away.

Percy Bysshe Shelley

If you have wrestled for a moment or two you will see the problem. The first three lines are plain sailing, of course: ABA. 'Frown' is something of a surprise; admittedly it sounds more like 'stone' than, say, 'sand' does, but it is a *half-rhyme* at best. Still, ABAB is what we are expecting, so let us for the moment accept 'frown' and 'stone' as rhymes; after all, 'frown' certainly does not rhyme with anything else in the poem! 'Command' presents another worry. Is it meant to half-rhyme with 'sand'? (Anyone who comes from Lancashire, as I do, might well claim it rhymes completely!) Another A rhyme? Nothing later rhymes with it. Perhaps we ought to call it C; after all, the next two alternate lines rhyme perfectly well: 'read; fed'. But line 7 ('things') clearly has to be E. So far we have ABAB CDED. 'Appear' is F, but 'kings' rhymes back and is E. The last four lines are orthodox: GHGH. Or are they? Does 'despair' (line 10) half-rhyme back with 'appear' (line 9)?

Confused? If you accept all possible half-rhymes, you end

up with ABABACDCEDEFEF. If you are really strict about rhyme, you get ABACDEFEGEHIHI. Either way, you do not end up with a rhyme scheme that makes much sense. It is clear, however, that there are some rhyming parts of the poem, and as it has fourteen lines you expect it to be some sort of sonnet. To a reader who is inexperienced in these forms, the oddness of the rhyme scheme may not be striking; to others it may be distinctly disconcerting.

- But what does the poem have to say?
- Look at the description of the statue in the first eight lines. What aspects of it are stressed by the poet?
- What do we learn of the relation between the sculptor and his subject?

Despite the vagaries of its rhyme scheme, the poem is surely intended to be a sonnet. As you might expect, the last six lines, the sestet, introduce a new way of looking at the subject of the poem.

- In what way does the poem alter its direction?
- What is the link between the inscription on the pedestal and the last three lines of the poem?
- Read the last three lines out loud and think about their sound. How does Shelley use sound to support the sense of the lines?

'Ozymandias' is a very individualistic use of the sonnet form. How successful it is depends of course on personal taste. You could claim that Shelley boldly refused to be tied down by the conventions of sonnet writing. You might also think that he lacked the patience to take care over his technique. The question remains: in your opinion has Shelley made full use of the opportunities provided by the form he chose to use as a vehicle for expressing his ideas?

The next sonnet, written by Gerard Manley Hopkins in the latter part of the nineteenth century, is at first even more surprising.

The Windhover

To Christ our Lord

I caught this morning morning's minion, king-
    dom of daylight's dauphin, dapple-dawn-drawn
        Falcon, in his riding
      Of the rolling level underneath him steady air, and
        striding
High there, how he rung upon the rein of a wimpling
    wing
5   In his ecstasy! then off, off forth on swing,
      As a skate's heel sweeps smooth on a bow-bend: the
        hurl and gliding
      Rebuffed the big wind. My heart in hiding
Stirred for a bird, – the achieve of, the mastery of the
    thing!

Brute beauty and valour and act, oh, air, pride,
    plume, here
10 Buckle! AND the fire that breaks from thee then, a
    billion
Times told lovelier, more dangerous, O my chevalier!

      No wonder of it: shéer plód makes plough down
        sillion
Shine, and blue-bleak embers, ah my dear,
    Fall, gall themselves, and gash gold-vermilion.

                  Gerard Manley Hopkins

The first thing that may strike you about this sonnet is that
it occupies twenty-two lines of print rather than fourteen. True –
but it is still a sonnet. The illusion of its having more lines than
it should is created by the way it is printed on the page. 'Line
1' of the poem stretches down to 'dapple-dawn-drawn' on line

2 of the print. The capital letter of 'Falcon' shows the start of 'line 2'. The sense of the unusual is increased when you take in the fact that 'line 1' has twenty-one syllables, whereas 'line 2' has six – not what you would call a regular metre. The same effects are to be found later in the poem; the line that begins 'As a skate's heel' also occupies two lines of print. Another interesting aspect of this poem is its rhyme scheme. The octave uses the same '-ing' rhyme throughout, although curiously in 'line 1' the word 'kingdom' is broken in half to provide a rhyme in the middle of the line rather than at the end. The sestet is more conventional in its use of alternate rhymes, although finding two different words to rhyme with 'billion' must be considered quite a feat on Hopkins's part! Despite the poem's initially surprising appearance on the page, the form of the Italian sonnet is unmistakable here.

Look at the way the poem splits up into the two traditional sections of an Italian sonnet, the octave and the sestet.

- What ideas hold the first eight lines together?
- How does the sestet change the direction of the poem?

You may well find some the phrasing of this poem difficult to get to grips with at first. Partly this could be because of some of the unusual words Hopkins uses – words such as 'wimpling' or 'sillion'. He also expresses himself at times in a very compact way; this quality of *compression* is one which gives poetry its distinctiveness. Prose can be ponderous in expressing ideas. Take that phrase early on in the poem, 'kingdom of daylight's dauphin' (line 1), and turn it to the word order of prose: 'the dauphin of the kingdom of daylight'. It seems clumsy. Poetry often twists around the order of words we have come to expect. This technique, known as *inversion*, can be used for the sake of compactness; it can also ensure that a rhyme-word appears at the end of a line. In the sonnet by Keats previously looked at (page 18), you can see how in line 4 the word 'hold' is shifted out of its normal position so that it can rhyme with 'bold' three lines later. Hopkins also has a way of piling words up on top of one another to suggest the intensity of his feelings: 'Brute beauty and valour and act, oh, air, pride, plume' (line 9). This is a demanding poem to read and come to terms with; part of that demand comes from the form that Hopkins chose to use.

- One final question – what do you make of the subtitle of the poem?
- How does it tie in with the experience related in the first part of the poem and the shift in emphasis which occurs in the second?

A Shilling Life

A shilling life will give you all the facts:
How Father beat him, how he ran away,
What were the struggles of his youth, what acts
Made him the greatest figure of his day:
5 Of how he fought, fished, hunted, worked all night,
Though giddy, climbed new mountains; named a sea:
Some of the last researchers even write
Love made him weep his pints like you and me.

With all his honours on, he sighed for one
10 Who, say astonished critics, lived at home;
Did little jobs about the house with skill
And nothing else; could whistle; would sit still
Or potter round the garden; answered some
Of his long marvellous letters but kept none.

W H Auden

So far, all the sonnets we have looked at were written before the twentieth century, which might imply that the form is one which is dying out. In fact, many modern poets have taken on the challenge of writing sonnets. 'A Shilling Life' by W H Auden is just one example.

The relative modernity of this poem (it was written in the mid-1930s) reveals itself mainly in its choice of vocabulary. We have already met the term poetic diction (page 19) when looking at Keats's sonnet. The concept that there is one vocabulary suitable for poetry and quite another for ordinary speech is one that has largely broken down during the course of this century, Auden, for example, in this poem writes of one who 'did little jobs about the house' and used to 'potter round the garden'. This use of everyday, *colloquial* language is looked at later in the book (page 47). For the moment, consider this poem as an example of a sonnet.

- Look at its rhyme scheme; what kind of sonnet is it?
- Does it contain a *volta*, a change in direction; how does its shape fit the ideas it expresses?
- How effective is the colloquial language? Does Auden have a particular purpose in using such terms as 'weep his pints like you and me'?

To end this chapter, here are four more sonnets. In each case, write a short critical appreciation. Decide what sort of sonnet you are dealing with (since Shakespeare wrote the last one it could be fairly obvious in this case!). Look at the rhyme scheme, the shape of the poem. Consider also, of course, what the poem has to say. How does the form of the poem help the poet to express his or her ideas in an effective way? How is the marriage of form and idea achieved?

Remember

Remember me when I am gone away.
   Gone far away into the silent land;
   When you can no more hold me by the hand,
Nor I half turn to go yet turning stay.
5   Remember me when no more day by day
   You tell me of our future that you planned.
   Only remember me; you understand
It will be late to counsel then or pray.
Yet if you should forget me for a while
10   And afterwards remember, do not grieve:
   For if the darkness and corruption leave
   A vestige of the thoughts that once I had,
Better by far you should forget and smile
   Than that you should remember and be sad.

Christina Rossetti

If thou must love me

If thou must love me, let it be for naught
   Except for love's sake only. Do not say,
   'I love her for her smile – her look – her way
Of speaking gently, – for a trick of thought
5   That falls in well with mine, and certes brought
   A sense of pleasant ease on such a day' –
   For these things in themselves, Beloved, may
Be changed, or change for thee – and love, so wrought,
May be unwrought so. Neither love me for
10   Thine own dear pity's wiping my cheeks dry:
   A creature might forget to weep, who bore
   Thy comfort long, and lose thy love thereby!
But love me for love's sake, that evermore
   Thou mayst love on, through love's eternity.

Elizabeth Barrett Browning

14 lines

Iambic Pentameter

Petrarcan used since
Tudor times

8 lines or octave
followed by sestet
volta - change

Character - 3 quatrain's
+ a couplet ababcdcdefef gg
Shakespearian

MW - Common

- Consider for a moment these two poems side by side. Do they have anything particularly in common? Which one do you find the more compelling? For what reasons?

To the Sad Moon

With how sad steps, O Moon, thou climb'st the skies!
  How silently, and with how wan a face!
  What! may it be that even in heavenly place
That busy archer his sharp arrows tries?
5 Sure, if that long-with-love-acquainted eyes
  Can judge of love, thou feel'st a lover's case:
  I read it in thy looks; thy languished grace
To me, that feel the like, thy state descries.
Then, even of fellowship, O Moon, tell me,
10 Is constant love deemed there but want of wit?
Are beauties there as proud as here they be?
  Do they above love to be loved, and yet
    Those lovers scorn whom that love doth
      possess?
  Do they call 'virtue' there – ungratefulness?

Sir Philip Sidney

- Both the previous sonnets were written around the middle of the nineteenth century, whereas Sir Philip Sidney was one of the most famous of Elizabethans and wrote in the later part of the sixteenth century. What features of his poem would tell you that it was from a much earlier age?
- The last poem in this chapter is another Shakespearian sonnet. When you write about this poem, look back also to 'That time of year . . .' (page 21). What features show them to be the work of the same poet?

How like a winter

How like a winter hath my absence been
   From thee, the pleasure of the fleeting year!
What freezings have I felt, what dark days seen!
   What old December's bareness everywhere!
5 And yet this time removed was summer's time,
   The teeming autumn, big with rich increase,
Bearing the wanton burden of the prime,
   Like widowed wombs after their lords' decease:
Yet this abundant issue seemed to me
10   But hope of orphans and unfathered fruit;
For summer and his pleasures wait on thee,
   And, thou away, the very birds are mute.
     Or, if they sing, 'tis with so dull a cheer,
     That leaves look pale, dreading the winter's near.

William Shakespeare

34

3   Images

Daffodils

I wandered lonely as a cloud
    That floats on high o'er vales and hills,
When all at once I saw a crowd,
    A host, of golden daffodils;
5   Beside the lake, beneath the trees,
Fluttering and dancing in the breeze.

Continuous as the stars that shine
    And twinkle on the Milky Way,
They stretched in never-ending line
10   Along the margin of a bay:
Ten thousand saw I at a glance,
Tossing their heads in sprightly dance.

The waves beside them danced, but they
    Out-did the sparkling waves in glee:
15   A poet could not but be gay,
    In such a jocund company:
I gazed – and gazed – but little thought
What wealth the show to me had brought:

For oft, when on my couch I lie
20   In vacant or in pensive mood,
They flash upon that inward eye
    Which is the bliss of solitude;
And then my heart with pleasure fills,
And dances with the daffodils.

William Wordsworth

Dotted throughout the first two chapters of this book you will find the word 'image' or 'imagery'. In this chapter I want to look a little more closely at what imagery is and how it works. This is a big subject, of course, and what we look at here may be thought of as scratching the surface. Generations of literary critics have argued about definitions of imagery and have produced hosts of terms to classify its different types. Literally an image is a representation or imitation of something which is real – already you can begin to feel the ground slip from under your feet as you wonder how you would define what is 'real'! In poetry, imagery at its simplest might be said to consist of using words to create a picture in the mind. To see this process at work, let us look first at the poem on page 35 which almost everyone half-knows, even if only from television advertisements!

The first two *stanzas* of this poem (to use the Italian word, which is a more specific description of a separate group of lines within a poem than, say, 'verses' would be), concentrate on evoking a picture of the daffodils – their colour, their numbers and their movement. To do this, Wordsworth uses several images. The daffodils are presented as a 'crowd', a 'host' (lines 3–4). They are given human characteristics; they are described as 'Tossing their heads in sprightly dance' (line 12). They appear to have human emotions: they 'Out-did the sparkling waves in glee' (line 14). The freshness and the vitality of the scene made a great impression on the poet; he seeks to recreate the experience for himself and for the reader. The ability to do this is reflected upon in the last two stanzas.

- Look at stanzas 3 and 4. What is the 'wealth' referred to in line 18?
- What experience is Wordsworth describing in the last stanza?

There are many different kinds of imagery, but the three most commonly encountered in poetry are *personification, simile* and *metaphor*. Personification has already been mentioned (page 8). In the sonnet by John Donne quoted in the previous chapter (page 24), personification is used so that something abstract, death in this case, can be given a physical presence and addressed as if it were a person. Wordsworth uses a variation on this technique when he describes the flowers as dancing.

Simile, as the word suggests, consists simply of likening one thing to another. The comparison is introduced by 'like' or 'as'. Wordsworth describes himself as wandering 'lonely as a cloud' (line 1).

Metaphor is another word which has been much argued about, but essentially it too involves a comparison, although not introduced by 'like'. The comparison involves the identification of one thing with another, so that the two merge together. For example, you might say of a boy who is a greedy and messy eater: 'he eats like a pig'. Here you would be using a simile. If however you said: 'The boy is a pig when he eats' you would be using a metaphor; for the brief moment of the comparison, boy and pig have become one and the same. In the last stanza of the poem, Wordsworth writes of his 'inward eye', by which we assume he means his imagination, which like an eye has the power of 'seeing' – but metaphorically, not literally.

Metaphors can flash briefly in a poem and then disappear again, but sometimes they can be sustained throughout its length, as in the next poem.

The Wiper

Through purblind night the wiper
Reaps a swathe of water
On the screen; we shudder on
 And hardly hold the road,
5 All we can see a segment
Of blackly shining asphalt
With the wiper moving across it
 Clearing, blurring, clearing.

But what to say of the road?
10 The monotony of its hardly
Visible camber, the mystery
 Of its far invisible margins,
Will these be always with us,
The night being broken only
15 By lights that pass or meet us
 From others in moving boxes?

Boxes of glass and water,
Upholstered, equipped with dials
Professing to tell the distance
20 We have gone, the speed we are going,
But never a gauge nor needle
To tell us where we are going
 Or when day will come, supposing
 This road exists in daytime.

25 For now we cannot remember
Where we were when it was not
Night, when it was not raining,
 Before this car moved forward
And the wiper backward and forward
30 Lighting so little before us
Of a road that, crouching forward,
 We watch move always towards us,

Which through the tiny segment
Cleared and blurred by the wiper
35   Is sucked in under the axle
        To be spewed behind us and lost
        While we, dazzled by darkness,
        Haul the black future towards us
        Peeling the skin from our hands;
40   And yet we hold the road.

Louis MacNeice

A first reading of this poem establishes some points clearly. What is being described is obviously a car journey through a wet night. The details supplied in the first two stanzas create the picture of the wet road, 'the blackly shining asphalt' (line 6) and the darkness of the surrounding countryside, the 'far invisible margins' (line 12). Gradually it becomes clear, however, that the poet is treating the subject from a different viewpoint from that of someone simply recalling a journey. For a start, the poem is written in the first person plural; it uses 'we' not 'I': 'we shudder on' (line 3); 'All we can see' (line 5). The reader and the poet are united in that they share the same predicament; they are both travelling down the same dark road. The second stanza widens the subject out: 'But what to say of the road?' Strange questions begin to obtrude on our consciousness. Will the road 'be always with us, (line 13)? How do we know 'where we are going' (line 22)? Are we right in 'supposing/This road exists in daytime' (lines 23–24)? – a question which takes us far beyond the secure and comfortable world of road maps and the A.A. In the last two stanzas the poem moves on to a time when 'we cannot remember/Where we were when it was not/Night' (lines 25–27). The description of the journey takes on a nightmare quality in which the road is 'sucked in under the axle/To be spewed behind us' (lines 35–36). The next three lines make it clear that the poet is not just talking about motoring:

39

> While we, dazzled by darkness,
> Haul the black future towards us
> Peeling the skin from our hands
> > (lines 37–39).

- Look back over the poem and consider its use of metaphor.
- The journey is an image, representing something else. What?
- MacNeice describes cars as 'equipped with dials/Professing to tell the distance/ We have gone'. What is the force of that word 'professing'?
- What use does MacNeice make of the image of the wiper?
- What point is he making in the last line?

One particular phrase in this poem illustrates another kind of poetic device. The phrase is 'dazzled by darkness' (line 37); the device of *paradox*. In poetry, paradox generally consists of statements or images which at first seem illogical or contradictory, but which when considered more closely can be said to yield up some truth. A whole poem can be founded on a paradox. Consider, for instance, the sonnet by John Donne in the last chapter (page 24). The idea that death is nothing to be feared, since it resembles a refreshing sleep, is developed in this poem. Donne ends by claiming that Death itself will die. The argument is not altogether convincing logically (after all, if death is nothing to be feared, why threaten Death with it?), but it carries great emotional force. The more ingenious and paradoxical the argument becomes, the more we are aware of the poet's struggle to convince himself. MacNeice's image of being 'dazzled by darkness' is less ambitious, but it is more arresting than 'blinded by darkness' would have been: it makes the reader stop and think.

The habit of finding significance in everyday experience, such as a car journey, is characteristic of the poet. In this next poem, Larkin seizes on the most commonplace of actions.

As Bad as a Mile

Watching the shied core
Striking the basket, skidding across the floor,
Shows less and less of luck, and more and more

Of failure spreading back up the arm
5   Earlier and earlier, the unraised hand calm,
The apple unbitten in the palm.

Philip Larkin

We have all known that moment of slight embarrassment when the apple core, lobbed with a casual flick of the wrist towards the waste-paper basket, bounces off it and on to the floor. Our attempt to demonstrate our mastery over inanimate objects ends with a humiliating second attempt, this time from much closer range! The experience can be especially galling when someone else has just performed the trick with arrogant ease.

- Consider how Larkin uses the image of the missed throw.
- What does he mean by 'failure spreading back up the arm' (line 4)?
- Does the idea of the unbitten apple remind you of anything?
- What is the point of the title of the poem?
- How seriously are we meant to take Larkin's view of this seemingly trivial incident?

The next poem, by Wilfred Owen, also uses an extended image as its basis, although in this case the image changes in the middle.

41

Miners

There was a whispering in my hearth,
    A sigh of the coal,
Grown wistful of a former earth
    It might recall.

5   I listened for a tale of leaves
        And smothered ferns;
Frond-forests; and the low, sly lives
        Before the fawns.

My fire might show steam-phantoms simmer
10   From Time's old cauldron,
Before the birds made nests in summer,
        Or men had children.

But the coals were murmuring of their mine,
        And moans down there
15   Of boys that slept wry sleep, and men
        Writhing for air.

And I saw white bones in the cinder-shard.
        Bones without number;
For many hearts with coal are charred
20   And few remember.

I thought of some who worked dark pits
        Of war, and died
Digging the rock where Death reputes
        Peace lies indeed.
25   Comforted years will sit soft-chaired
        In rooms of amber;
The years will stretch their hands, well-cheered
        By our lives' ember.

> The centuries will burn rich loads
> 30   With which we groaned,
> Whose warmth shall lull their dreaming lids
>   While songs are crooned.
> But they will not dream of us poor lads
>   Lost in the ground.

Wilfred Owen

The name of Wilfred Owen may well evoke immediate thoughts of the First World War. Owen served in it as an officer, fought in the trenches, and was killed in action just a few days before the Armistice. His most famous poems, such as 'Dulce et Decorum', bring out in vivid detail the horror of trench warfare. At first, however, this poem does not seem to be about the war at all.

- Look at the first five stanzas. How does Owen use the image of sitting in front of the fire to develop his thoughts about miners? What is the point of the reference to 'a former earth' (line 3)?
- What exactly are the 'bones' that the poet sees?
- How does Owen appeal to the sense of hearing as well as sight?

In the sixth stanza there is a shift in the direction of the poem, rather like the *volta* in the Italian sonnets of the last chapter. Now Owen presents miners in a metaphorical sense, as those who dig 'dark pits of war'.

- Follow up that metaphor.
- Why were these 'miners' digging?
- What, according to Owen, did they hope to find?

Owen described the last few lines of the poem as 'oh, so bitter'. They make very striking use of the device of personification.

- How does personification bring out the bitterness of Owen's thought in the last two stanzas?

This poem is also interesting from a purely technical point of view. In discussing the rhyme scheme of Shelley's sonnet 'Ozymandias' (page 26), we noted some line endings that were almost rhymes but not quite, and wondered whether they were deliberate or not. In 'Miners' there is no doubt. One of the techniques for which Owen's poetry has become well-known is his use of *half-rhyme*. If you look at the rhyme scheme of 'Miners' you will see that it uses an ABAB pattern. The rhymes themselves are often of the 'nearly but not quite' variety. For example, the second stanza rhymes 'leaves' and 'lives', 'ferns' and 'fawns'. 'True' rhyme works on the basis of using identical vowel *and* consonant sounds: 'core – floor – more', for example, in 'As Bad as a Mile' (page 41). Owen, on the other hand, uses the same consonants but varies the vowel sounds, so that in the seventh stanza 'chaired' can rhyme with 'cheered', 'amber' with 'ember'. This gentle, lilting rhyme gives the poem its dreamy quality, against which are placed the harsh realities of war and death.

When we think of *alliteration*, we often tend to think of the tongue-twisters of childhood: 'Round the rugged rocks/ The ragged rascals ran'. Like rhyme, alliteration has the advantage of being memorable and is often used in mnemonics, little jingles to help us remember things. But alliteration is also a device for serious poetry. In fact, most poetry in England before the Norman Conquest of 1066 used alliteration as its basis, and one of the greatest poems of Middle English (that is to say the English of the Middle Ages), carried on that tradition. *Sir Gawayn and the Green Knight*, written in the later part of the fourteenth century, at roughly the same time as Chaucer was writing *The Canterbury Tales*, opens as follows:

Sithen the sege and the assaut was sesed at Troye
The borgh brittened and brent to brondes and askes,
The tulk that the trammes of tresoun ther wrought,
Was tried for his trecherie, the trewest on erthe.

A very literal translation might be:

After the siege and the assault was ceased at Troy,
The city destroyed and burnt to brands and ashes,
The man who the plots of treason there made,
Stood revealed in his treachery, the clearest on earth.

As you can see from the original, the poetry relies for its coherent pattern upon alliteration, the repetition of consonant sounds such as *s* in the first line, *b* or *br* in the second, *t* or *tr* in the third and fourth. As you can imagine, this style of writing demanded a very high degree of technical skill; in the case of *Sir Gawayn*, alliteration had to be sustained for over 2,500 lines!

In the remaining five poems of this chapter, all relatively modern, a central image, or series of images, is dominant. The first, by W H Auden, is a reflection on a visit to an art gallery in Brussels. In a sense, this poem is about images, since it is concerned with the way the Old Masters, the great painters of the past, treat in their pictures the subject of human suffering. In the second stanza, Auden directs our attention to one specific painting, Peter Brueghel's *The Fall of Icarus*. The Greek legend tells how the young man Icarus was given a pair of wings with which he was able to fly. Alas, in his joy he flew too near the sun; the wax which held the wings together melted and he was pitched into the sea to drown. Brueghel's picture shows the falling boy entering the water. In the foreground is a headland, where a farmer ploughs the land.

Musée des Beaux Arts

About suffering they were never wrong,
The Old Masters: how well they understood
Its human position; how it takes place
While someone else is eating or opening a window or
    just walking dully along;
5 How, when the aged are reverently, passionately
    waiting
For the miraculous birth, there always must be
Children who did not specially want it to happen,
    skating
On a pond at the edge of the wood:
10 They never forgot
That even the dreadful martyrdom must run its
    course
Anyhow in a corner, some untidy spot
Where the dogs go on with their doggy life and the
    torturer's horse
Scratches its innocent behind on a tree.

15 In Brueghel's *Icarus*, for instance: how everything
    turns away
Quite leisurely from the disaster; the ploughman
    may
Have heard the splash, the forsaken cry.
But for him it was not an important failure; the sun
    shone
As it had to on the white legs disappearing into the
    green
20 Water; and the expensive delicate ship that must
    have seen
Something amazing, a boy falling out of the sky,
Had somewhere to get to and sailed calmly on.

W H Auden

- What contrasts does Auden stress in the first stanza?
- How does he use the image of Brueghel's *Icarus* to reinforce his belief that the Old Masters were never wrong about suffering?
- Do you agree with the views the poet puts forward here?
- The style of this poem is very distinctive, with its relaxed, conversational tone. Comment on how this is achieved.
- Despite its break about two-thirds of the way through, this poem may at first sight seem shapeless. Is it?

The next poem, by Hugh MacDiarmid, moves even further from the highly structured verse of a poem like 'Miners'. It uses imagery, however, in a way that is deeply poetic.

Crystals like Blood

I remember how, long ago, I found
Crystals like blood in a broken stone.

I picked up a broken chunk of bed-rock
And turned it this way and that,
5   It was heavier than one would have expected
From its size. One face was caked
With brown limestone. But the rest
Was a hard greenish-grey quartz-like stone
Faintly dappled with darker shadows,
10 And in this quartz ran veins and beads
Of bright magenta.

And I remember how later on I saw
How mercury is extracted from cinnebar
– The double ring of iron piledrivers
15 Like the multiple legs of a fantastically symmetrical
spider
Rising and falling with monotonous precision,

Marching round in an endless circle
And pounding up and down with a tireless, thunderous
force,
While, beyond, another conveyor drew the crumbled ore
20 From the bottom and raised it to an opening high
In the side of a gigantic grey-white kiln.

So I remember how mercury is got
When I contrast my living memory of you
And your dear body rotting here in the clay
25 – And feel once again released in me
The bright torrents of felicity, naturalness, and faith
My treadmill memory draws from you yet.

Hugh MacDiarmid

This poem opens quietly, with its recollection of a stone found
on a beach, long ago. The third stanza shows just how far
poets of the twentieth century have moved away from the
concept of poetic diction (see page 19), in its description of
the process by which mercury is extracted from cinnabar. In
the last stanza, the two recollections are drawn together by a
third, one which suddenly and surprisingly releases great
depths of feeling, through the power of imagery.

- Look at the description of the stone in the first two stanzas.
  What qualities of the image does the poet stress?
- In third stanza, what particular qualities of this process are
  brought out?
- How are these two ideas united in the last stanza? Is its
  emotional charge totally unexpected or are there any hints
  earlier in the poem of what is to come?
- How do you react to the style of the poem? In what ways
  does it resemble or differ from Auden's in 'Musée des Beaux
  Arts'?

After two poems which use a more conversational tone and
varying line lengths, we go back to something rather stricter
in this poem by Philip Larkin.

Ambulances

Closed like confessionals, they thread
Loud noons of cities, giving back
None of the glances they absorb.
Light glossy grey, arms on a plaque,
5   They come to rest at any kerb:
All streets in time are visited.

Then children strewn ón steps or road,
Or women coming from the shops
Past smells of different dinners, see
10   A wild white face that overtops
Red stretcher-blankets momently
As it is carried in and stowed,

And sense the solving emptiness
That lies just under all we do,
15   And for a second get it whole,
So permanent and blank and true.
The fastened doors recede. *Poor soul*,
They whisper at their own distress;

For borne away in deadened air
20   May go the sudden shut of loss
Round something nearly at an end,
And what cohered in it across
The years, the unique random blend
Of families and fashions, there

25   At last begin to loosen. Far
From the exchange of love to lie
Unreachable inside a room
The traffic parts to let go by
Brings closer what is left to come,
30   And dulls to distance all we are.

Philip Larkin

In the first two stanzas, Larkin frequently uses description. Look at the details he chooses to pick out.

- Why are ambulances 'like confessionals' (line 1)?
- What point is made by 'All streets in time are visited' (line 6)?
- What does Larkin stress through description in the second stanza?

The third stanza moves away from the visual image of the ambulance and begins to consider the more abstract reality that it stands for – the reality of death.

- In what way do the onlookers 'sense the solving empti-ness/That lies just under all we do' (lines 13–14)?
- Why do they whisper 'at their own distress' (line 18)?

The last two stanzas form the most difficult part of the poem, because here Larkin mixes abstract and concrete images in his effort to convey what the process of dying is like. Also there are problems of *syntax* here. By syntax, I mean the way that words and phrases are organised into complete sentences. The two sentences which end the poem are both quite long and involved; some care is needed in working out how the different phrases fit together within them.

- Comment on the last two stanzas. How do they seek to achieve their effect? How successful are they?
- Why, do you think, does Larkin use more complicated syntax here?
- Look at the shape of the poem. What strikes you about it?

The last two poems in this chapter both have a single central image, with other imagery worked into them. They are presented without commentary, but with some questions which you might wish to think about as you write an appreciation of them.

The Arrival of the Bee Box

I ordered this, this clean wood box
Square as a chair and almost too heavy to lift.
I would say it was the coffin of a midget
Or a square baby
5   Were there not such a din in it.

The box is locked, it is dangerous.
I have to live with it overnight
And I can't keep away from it.
There are no windows, so I can't see what is in
    there.
10   There is only a little grid, no exit.

I put my eye to the grid.
It is dark, dark,
With the swarmy feeling of African hands
Minute and shrunk for export,
15   Black on black, angrily clambering.

How can I let them out?
It is the noise that appals me most of all,
The unintelligible syllables.
It is like a Roman mob,
20   Small, taken one by one, but my god, together!

I lay my ear to furious Latin.
I am not a Caesar.
I have simply ordered a box of maniacs.
They can be sent back.
25   They can die, I need feed them nothing, I am the
    owner.

I wonder how hungry they are.
I wonder if they would forget me
If I just undid the locks and stood back and turned into
    a tree.
There is the laburnum, its blond colonnades,
30 And the petticoats of the cherry.

They might ignore me immediately
In my moon suit and funeral veil.
I am no source of honey
So why should they turn on me?
35 Tomorrow I will be sweet God, I will set them free.

The box is only temporary.

Sylvia Plath

- Consider the speaker's changes of attitude to the box and its contents as the poem develops. How does imagery bring them out?
- What do you make of the last line?
- Why is it set apart from the rest?
- Does it in any way make you re-think your interpretation of the central image of this poem?

The Building

Higher than the handsomest hotel
The lucent comb shows up for miles, but see,
All round it close-ribbed streets rise and fall
Like a great sigh out of the last century.
5 The porters are scruffy; what keep drawing up
At the entrance are not taxis; and in the hall
As well as creepers hangs a frightening smell.

There are paperbacks, and tea at so much a cup,
Like an airport lounge, but those who tamely sit

10   On rows of steel chairs turning the ripped mags
      Haven't come far. More like a local bus,
      These outdoor clothes and half-filled shopping bags
      And faces restless and resigned, although
      Every few minutes comes a kind of nurse

15   To fetch someone away: the rest refit
      Cups back to saucers, cough, or glance below
      Seats for dropped gloves or cards. Humans, caught
      On ground curiously neutral, homes and names
      Suddenly in abeyance; some are young,
20   Some old, but most at that vague age that claims
      The end of choice, the last of hope; and all

      Here to confess that something has gone wrong.
      It must be error of a serious sort,
      For see how many floors it needs, how tall
25   It's grown by now, and how much money goes
      In trying to correct it. See the time,
      Half-past eleven on a working day,
      And these picked out of it; see, as they climb

      To their appointed levels, how their eyes
30   Go to each other, guessing; on the way
      Someone's wheeled past, in washed-to-rags ward clothes:
      They see him, too. They're quiet. To realise
      This new thing held in common makes them quiet,
      For past these doors are rooms, and rooms past those,
35   And more rooms yet, each one further off

      And harder to return from; and who knows
      Which he will see, and when? For the moment, wait,
      Look down at the yard. Outside seems old enough:
      Red brick, lagged pipes, and someone walking by it
40   Out to the car park, free. Then, past the gate,
      Traffic; a locked church; short terraced streets
      Where kids chalk games, and girls with hair-dos fetch

Their separates from the cleaners – O world,
Your loves, your chances, are beyond the stretch
45 Of any hand from here! And so, unreal,
A touching dream to which we all are lulled
But wake from separately. In it, conceits
And self-protecting ignorance congeal
To carry life, collapsing only when

50 Called to these corridors (for now once more
The nurse beckons –). Each gets up and goes
At last. Some will be out by lunch, or four;
Others, not knowing it, have come to join
The unseen congregations whose white rows
55 Lie set apart above – women, men;
Old, young; crude facets of the only coin

This place accepts. All know they are going to die.
Not yet, perhaps not here, but in the end,
And somewhere like this. That is what it means,
60 This clean-sliced cliff; a struggle to transcend
The thought of dying, for unless its powers
Outbuild cathedrals nothing contravenes
The coming dark, though crowds each evening try

With wasteful, weak, propitiatory flowers.

Philip Larkin

- What physical details are stressed in the first three stanzas?
- What, according to Larkin, happens to people who go to hospitals?
- Why does he describe the view out of the window in stanzas 6 and 7?
- 'That is what it means,/ This clean-sliced cliff' (lines 59–60). What ultimately is the meaning of the central image of 'The Building'?

- There have been three examples of Philip Larkin's work in this chapter. What are your impressions of his preoccupations as a poet, and of his technique?

4 Variety of approach: animals

In the last chapter, we looked at poems which were dominated by varied central images. To continue the theme of the variety of ways in which poets approach their subjects, we look in this chapter at a number of poems which take as their starting points living things other than man. Two such poems have already featured in previous chapters. In 'The Windhover' (page 28), Hopkins writes of the hawk's mastery of the art of flying, and then goes on to express his sense of the unexpected wonders of creation. On the other hand, Sylvia Plath in 'The Arrival of the Bee Box' (page 51) feels disquiet, almost fear, rather than wonder. The first poem in this chapter uses the image of an owl in quite a different way.

If you compare this poem with that of Hopkins (page 28), you will see both similarities and differences in the way the two poets treat their subjects (although very little similarity in style). Both of them use the bird as a stimulus for other related thoughts. After Hopkins's ecstatic description of the hawk in flight, he moves away to images of fire and brightness; the owl's cry makes Thomas think of 'all who lay under the stars,/ Soldiers and poor, unable to rejoice' (lines 15–16).

- What differences do you notice in the way the two poets look at their subjects?
- What does Thomas mean when he says 'salted was my food, and my repose' (line 13)?
- How do you respond to this poem?

Edward Thomas wrote in the early part of the twentieth century; like Wilfred Owen, he was killed in the First World War.

The Owl

Downhill I came, hungry, and yet not starved;
Cold, yet had heat within me that was proof
Against the North wind; tired, yet so that rest
Had seemed the sweetest thing under a roof.

5   Then at the inn I had food, fire, and rest,
Knowing how hungry, cold, and tired was I.
All of the night was quite barred out except
An owl's cry, a most melancholy cry

Shaken out long and clear upon the hill,
10 No merry note, nor cause of merriment,
But one telling me plain what I escaped
And others could not, that night, as in I
    went.

And salted was my food, and my repose,
Salted and sobered, too, by the bird's voice
15 Speaking for all who lay under the stars,
Soldiers and poor, unable to rejoice.

Edward Thomas

The next poem is somewhat more contemporary and chooses what may seem an unusual subject. On reflection, it is not so much the subject of this poem that is unusual as its treatment. After all, snails had featured in poetry before Gunn wrote about one, but I doubt if they have ever been presented in the way they are here.

Considering the Snail

The snail pushes through a green
night, for the grass is heavy
with water and meets over
the bright path he makes, where rain
5 has darkened the earth's dark. He
moves in a wood of desire,

pale antlers barely stirring
as he hunts. I cannot tell
what power is at work, drenched there
10 with purpose, knowing nothing.
What is a snail's fury? All
I think is that if later

I parted the blades above
the tunnel and saw the thin
15 trail of broken white across
litter, I would never have
imagined the slow passion
to that deliberate progress.

Thom Gunn

- What words in this poem stand out as particularly striking?
- From what viewpoint does Gunn consider the snail here?
- How would you interpret the following lines: 'I cannot tell/ What power is at work, drenched there/ with purpose, knowing nothing' (lines 8–10)?
- A critic of Gunn's poetic style once wrote this poem out as if it were continuous prose. 'There you are,' he said. 'It makes not a scrap of difference.' Would you regard that as fair comment?

Any chapter on the treatment of the animal kingdom in poetry is bound to include the present Poet Laureate, Ted Hughes. Ever since his first volume of poems was published in 1957, this has been one of his major concerns.

Hawk Roosting

I sit in the top of the wood, my eyes closed.
Inaction, no falsifying dream
Between my hooked head and hooked feet:
Or in sleep rehearse perfect kills and eat.

5   The convenience of the high trees!
The air's buoyancy and the sun's ray
Are of advantage to me;
And the earth's face upward for my inspection.

My feet are locked upon the rough bark.
10   It took the whole of Creation
To produce my foot, my each feather:
Now I hold Creation in my foot

Or fly up, and revolve it all slowly –
I kill where I please because it is all mine.
15   There is no sophistry in my body:
My manners are tearing off heads –

The allotment of death.
For the one path of my flight is direct
Through the bones of the living.
20   No arguments assert my right:

The sun is behind me.
Nothing has changed since I began.
My eye has permitted no change.
I am going to keep things like this.

Ted Hughes

'Hawk Roosting', like 'The Windhover', takes a hawk as its subject. Hopkins viewed the bird in flight; Hughes' hawk is at rest. More importantly, in this poem the poet speaks through the hawk.

This poem provides a good opportunity to say something about *persona*, the poet's standpoint. The majority of the poems quoted in this book work on the basis of the poet using the first person and speaking in his own voice. Sometimes he is addressing the reader, as in Auden's 'Musée des Beaux Arts' (page 46); in 'Crystals like Blood' (page 47), the poet is ultimately speaking to his dead wife; in 'The Rejected Member's Wife' (page 3), one might say that the poet is talking to himself. However, not all the poems we have looked at worked in this way. For example, in 'This is Just to Say' (page 5), the poet seems to be speaking in his own person, but we are left to guess to whom or what circumstances.

- Look back over some of the poems previously quoted. In each case, ask yourself who is speaking, to whom and in what circumstances.

In 'Hawk Roosting', Hughes uses the first person, but it soon becomes clear that it is not the poet who speaks. He has adopted a persona, a mask which a classical actor once used to wear in order to perform a part in a play. In a sense you could say that this poem was a piece of dramatic verse: its voice is that of a character other than the author and the words are spoken within a particular context. It would make no sense if the reader were not aware of this.

Let us look first at some of the areas of possible difficulty in the poem. In the first stanza, we are told that the hawk's eyes closed. How, apparently, does a hawk's sleep differ from a human's? Explain the 'advantages' described in the second stanza. Look at lines 14–18. What point is the hawk making here? (You may need a dictionary for 'sophistry'; 'allotment' requires a little care too.)

- What is the significance of the statement 'The sun is behind me' (line 21)?
- When you have got to grips with the detail of the poem, think about the persona Hughes has adopted here. What is its character? What might be the human counterpart of Hughes's hawk?

The last poem in this chapter is also by Ted Hughes, but space only allows for a small sample of his brilliant exploration of the natural world. A look at some of his other work, poems such as 'Thrushes', 'Pike' or 'Thistles', would be well worth while.

The next poem also uses a persona, whose inclinations are stated pretty clearly in the title: 'Mort aux Chats' – 'Death to Cats!'

Mort aux Chats

There will be no more cats.
Cats spread infection,
cats pollute the air,
cats consume seven times
5   their own weight in food a week,
cats were worshipped in
decadent societies (Egypt
and Ancient Rome), the Greeks
had no use for cats. Cats
10   sit down to pee (our scientists
have proved it). The copulation
of cats is harrowing; they
are unbearably fond of the moon.
Perhaps they are all right in
15   their own country but their
traditions are alien to ours.
Cats smell, they can't help it,

you notice it going upstairs.
Cats watch too much television,
20 they can sleep through storms,
they stabbed us in the back
last time. There have never been
any great artists who were cats.
They don't deserve a capital C
25 except at the beginning of a sentence.
I blame my headache and my
plants dying on to cats.
Our district is full of them,
property values are falling.
30 When I dream of God I see
a Massacre of Cats. Why
should they insist on their own
language and religion, who
needs to purr to make his point?
35 Death to all cats! The Rule
of Dogs shall last a thousand years!

Peter Porter

This poem is an assembly of prejudices.

● Are they all equally extreme?
● Do some have more apparent logic than others?
● What differing kinds of human prejudice are represented here?
● 'The Rule of Dogs shall last a thousand years!' (line 36) Do you detect a historical reference here?
● What kind of poem is this? How does it differ from 'Hawk Roosting' in its use of a persona?

The next two poems take us back to the kind of poetry where the poet speaks directly to the reader. Both recall a distressing experience.

After Death

Opening up the house
After three weeks away
I found bird droppings
All over the ground floor,
5 White and heavy on the windows,
On the worktop,
On the cupboards,
On every wild hope of freedom.

I could not find any bird
10 At first, and feared
Some science fiction mystery,
To be horribly explained
As soon as whatever
It was felt sure
15 It had got me alone,
A mile from the village.

At last I discovered him,
Weightless and out of the running,
More null than old wrapping paper
20 A month after Christmas.
No food inside him, of course,
He had died of hunger
And no waste either,
He was quite empty.

25 His desperate ghost
Flew down my throat and my ears.
There was no air
He had not suffered in.
He lay in one place,
30 His droppings were everywhere
More vivid, more terrible
Than he had been, ever.

Patricia Beer

- Look at the differing emotions conveyed in this poem. How does the poet give them force?
- How does this poem hold together? Could it just as well be written out as prose?

Interruption to a Journey

The hare we had run over
Bounced about the road
On the springing curve
Of its spine.

5 Cornfields breathed in the darkness,
We were going through the darkness and
The breathing cornfields from one
Important place to another.

We broke the hare's neck
10 And made that place, for a moment,
The most important place there was,
Where a bowstring was cut
And a bow broken forever
That had shot itself through so many
15 Darknesses and cornfields.

It was left in that landscape.
It left us in another.

Norman MacCaig

- How does the poem's title help to bring out its point?
- How does the poet create the scene here?
- The last two lines are very carefully balanced. What point do they make?
- Compare this poem with the last one. Which one do you more striking, and why?

The final three poems in this chapter are presented for written appreciation. As in the last chapter, some possible areas of discussion are suggested after each one. In the first, W B Yeats writes of a visit to Coole Park in County Galway. Many years before this poem was written, Yeats had stayed in the country house to which the park belonged.

The Wild Swans at Coole

The trees are in their autumn beauty,
The woodland paths are dry,
Under the October twilight the water
Mirrors a still sky;
5   Upon the brimming water among the stones
Are nine-and-fifty swans.

The nineteenth autumn has come upon me
Since I first made my count;
I saw, before I had well finished,
10 All suddenly mount
And scatter wheeling in great broken rings
Upon their clamorous wings.

I have looked upon those brilliant creatures,
And now my heart is sore.
15 All's changed since I, hearing at twilight,
The first time on this shore,
The bell-beat of their wings above my head,
Trod with a lighter tread.

Unwearied still, lover by lover,
20 They paddle in the cold
Companionable streams or climb the air;
Their hearts have not grown old;
Passion or conquest, wander where they will,
Attend upon them still.

25 But now they drift upon the still water,
    Mysterious, beautiful;
    Among what rushes will they build,
    By what lake's edge or pool
    Delight men's eyes when I awake some day
30 To find they have flown away?

W B Yeats

- How does Yeats create the atmosphere of the park and convey the beauty and mystery of the swans?
- How does he bring his personal feelings into the poem?

The next poem is by D H Lawrence, probably better known as a novelist but, like Thomas Hardy, also a prolific poet. Like Ted Hughes, he wrote a number of poems on subjects drawn from the natural world. Space only allows for one, but poems such as 'Hummingbird', 'Snake' and 'Baby Tortoise' are well worth seeking out.

Mountain Lion

Climbing through the January snow, into the Lobo
    Canyon
Dark grow the spruce-trees, blue is the balsam,
    water sounds still unfrozen, and the trail is still
    evident.

Men!
Two men!
5   Men! The only animal in the world to fear!

They hesitate
We hesitate
They have a gun.
We have no gun.

10   Then we all advance, to meet.

Two Mexicans, strangers, emerging out of the dark
and snow and inwardness of the Lobo valley.
What are they doing here on this vanishing trail?

What is he carrying?
Something yellow.
15   A deer?

Qué tiene, amigo?
León –

He smiles, foolishly, as if he were caught doing
    wrong.
And we smile, foolishly, as if we didn't know.
20   He is quite gentle and dark-faced.

It is a mountain lion,
A long, long slim cat, yellow like a lioness.
Dead.

He trapped her this morning, he says, smiling
    foolishly.
25   Lift up her face,
Her round, bright face, bright as frost.
Her round, fine-fashioned head, with two dead ears;
And stripes in the brilliant frost of her face, sharp,
    fine dark rays,
Dark, keen, fine rays in the brilliant frost of her
    face.
30   Beautiful dead eyes.

Hermoso es!

They go out towards the open;
We go on into the gloom of Lobo.
And above the trees I found her lair,
35   A hole in the blood-orange brilliant rocks that stick
     up, a little cave.
And bones, and twigs, and a perilous ascent.

So, she will never leap up that way again, with the
     yellow flash of a mountain lion's long shoot!
And her bright striped frost-face will never watch
     any more, out of the shadow of the cave in the
     blood-orange rock,
Above the trees of the Lobo dark valley-mouth!

40 Instead, I look out.
And out to the dim of the desert, like a dream,
     never real;
To the snow of the Sangre de Cristo mountains, the
     ice of the mountains of Picoris,
And near across at the opposite steep of snow, green
     trees motionless standing in snow, like a
     Christmas toy.

And I think in this empty world there was room for
     me and a mountain lion.
45 And I think in the world beyond, how easily we
     might spare a million or two of humans
And never miss them.
Yet what a gap in the world, the missing white
     frost-face of that slim yellow mountain lion!

D H Lawrence

For those who are uncertain of the Spanish in the poem, the
exchange in lines 16–17 means 'What have you got, my
friend?' – 'A lion – '. Line 31 means 'It is beautiful'.

- There are two meetings in this poem: man and man, man and lion. How is the distinctive quality of each brought out?
- How do you react to what Lawrence has to say in the last stanza of the poem?
- What do you make of Lawrence's technique as a writer of poetry?

An Otter

I

Underwater eyes, an eel's
Oil of water body, neither fish nor beast is the otter:
Four-legged yet water-gifted, to outfish fish;
With webbed feet and long ruddering tail
5   And a round head like an old tomcat.

Brings the legend of himself
From before wars or burials, in spite of hounds and
    vermin-poles;
Does not take root like the badger. Wanders, cries;
Gallops along land he no longer belongs to;
10   Re-enters the water by melting.

Of neither water nor land. Seeking
Some world lost when first he dived, that he
    cannot come at since,
Takes his changed body into the holes of lakes;
As if blind, cleaves the stream's push till he
    licks
15   The pebbles of the source; from sea

To sea crosses in three nights
Like a king in hiding. Crying to the old shape of
    the starlit land,
Over sunken farms where the bats go round,
Without answer. Till light and birdsong come
20   Walloping up roads with the milk wagon.

II

The hunt's lost him. Pads on mud,
Among sedges, nostrils a surface bead,
The otter remains, hours. The air,
Circling the globe, tainted and necessary,

25   Mingling tobacco-smoke, hounds and parsley,
Comes carefully to the sunk lungs.
So the self under the eye lies,
Attendant and withdrawn. The otter belongs

In double robbery and concealment –
30   From water that nourishes and drowns, and from
         land
That gave him his length and the mouth of the
         hound.
He keeps fat in the limpid integument

Reflections live on. The heart beats thick,
Big trout muscle out of the dead cold;
35   Blood is the belly of logic; he will lick
The fishbone bare. And can take stolen hold

On a bitch otter in a field full
Of nervous horses, but linger nowhere.
Yanked above hounds, reverts to nothing at all,
40   To this long pelt over the back of a chair.

                                        Ted Hughes

This is probably the most difficult poem in the chapter. You
may not feel confident that you are clear about every detail.
If so, do not worry; it is a poem that has been much argued
about!

- Look at Part I of the poem. In line 11, the otter is described as being 'Of neither water nor land'. How is this quality developed here?

- There are many references to wandering and seeking. Explore this area of imagery. What is Hughes suggesting about the otter?

- Do all these images tell us anything about man as well as about otters?

- How does Part II link up with Part I? What new elements does it contain?

- Look carefully at Hughes' technique in this poem? Does he use any kind of rhyme scheme? What about the length of the lines?

- Is Part II simply a continuation in style from Part I, or do you see any differences?

- Both Lawrence and Hughes are greatly drawn to the natural world. From the evidence of these last two poems, how do they differ in their approach as poets? To which of these poems do you respond more strongly, and why?

5   The personal touch

The poems in this chapter cover quite a range of ages and styles, but they all have at least one quality in common: they are all very personal. In each of them, the poet speaks to someone or about someone. There are, of course, other examples of such poetry in this book. The two poems which begin it, 'Not Waving but Drowning' (page 1) and 'The Rejected Member's Wife' (page 3) are both good examples of poems about someone; 'Crystals like Blood' (page 47) or 'Since there's no help . . .' (page 22) show the poet addressing someone other than the reader. The following ten poems show the unique power possessed by poetry of expressing personal feeling in all the varied aspects of human contact. The first two, by Housman and Yeats, have in common their concern with the passage of time.

Keats's poem 'To Autumn' (page 6) raised the question of the importance or otherwise of biographical knowledge in the appreciation of poetry. Hardly surprisingly, the debate was not resolved; both sides have strong arguments. The same question can be raised about Housman's poem. The brief summary of Housman's life which can be found in *The Oxford Companion to English Literature* tells us that while he was at university in Oxford in the late 1870s, he 'formed a passionate attachment' to one of his fellow students. This homosexual love found no physical expression; its object later married and emigrated to India. This poem, written many years after the original experience, is Housman's wry reflection upon it.

- Does knowing something about the background of this poem alter your response to it? Is the knowledge a help or a hindrance?

Because I liked you better

Because I liked you better
    Than suits a man to say,
It irked you, and I promised
    To throw the thought away.

5 To put the world between us
    We parted, stiff and dry;
'Good-bye', said you, 'forget me.'
    'I will, no fear', said I.

If here, where clover whitens
10   The dead man's knoll, you pass,
And no tall flower to meet you
    Starts in the trefoiled grass,

Halt by the headstone naming
    The heart no longer stirred,
15 And say the lad that loved you
    Was one that kept his word.

A E Housman

One of Housman's distinctive qualities as a poet is his restrained, ironic *tone*. The word 'tone' is one which comes very frequently into discussion about poetry; it appeared, for example, in the consideration of Robert Frost's poem 'Out, Out – ' (page 10). As I said in the Introduction, I think it a good idea whenever possible to read a poem out loud, if you are to respond to it fully. Second best is to try to 'hear' the poem in your head as you read it. In either case, you will want to ask yourself what is the appropriate tone of voice to use. Your decision will depend on what you think the poet is trying to say to you and what his own attitude and feelings are about his subject.

- What are Housman's feelings here? What tone does he use to express them?
- What characterises Housman's technique in this poem?
- How does he use metre here?

Answering that last question might bring out the subject of *line-endings*. Traditionally these have been classed as *masculine* and *feminine*; you may well suspect such terms to be the products of a more innocent age! A feminine ending is one where the last syllable of the line is not stressed (strictly speaking, the syllable should be an extra one, an addition to the normal metrical pattern of the line). A masculine ending is one where the stress falls on the final syllable. If you look at Housman's poem, you will see that he alternates between the two kinds of endings, so that in the first stanza, for example, '*bet*ter' and '*prom*ised' end with an unstressed syllable, whereas 'to *say*' and 'a*way*' both have the stress on the the final syllable. When you read the poem out loud, you can hear how this alternating pattern gives each pair of lines a sense of completeness.

When you are old

When you are old and grey and full of sleep,
And nodding by the fire, take down this book,
And slowly read, and dream of the soft look
Your eyes had once, and of their shadows deep;

5   How many loved your moments of glad grace,
And loved your beauty with love false or true,
But one man loved the pilgrim soul in you,
And loved the sorrows of your changing face;

And bending down beside the glowing bars,
10 Murmur, a little sadly, how Love fled
And paced upon the mountains overhead
And hid his face amid a crowd of stars.

W B Yeats

- According to the poet, what was the essential difference between his love for the woman addressed in this poem, and that of others?
- What do you make of the last three lines of the poem? What do they portray?
- Compare this poem with the previous one. What similarities and differences do they have in what they say and how they say it?

The next poem takes us back to John Donne, one of whose 'Holy Sonnets' we have looked at earlier (page 24). 'Death, be not proud' was concerned with religious themes of death and salvation. Salvation comes into this poem too, but in a very different context.

The Apparition

When by thy scorn, O murderess, I am dead,
And that thou think'st thee free
From all solicitation from me,
Then shall my ghost come to thy bed,
5 And thee, fained vestal, in worse arms shall see;
Then thy sick taper will begin to wink,
And he, whose thou art then, being tired before,
Will, if thou stir, or pinch to wake him, think
    Thou call'st for more,
10 And in false sleep will from thee shrink,
And then, poor aspen wretch, neglected thou
Bathed in a cold quicksilver sweat wilt lie
    A verier ghost than I;
What I will say, I will not tell thee now,
15 Lest that preserve thee; and since my love is spent,
I had rather thou shouldst painfully repent,
Than by my threatenings rest still innocent.

John Donne

Most the language of this poem is clear and straightforward, although the reader needs to know that a 'fained vestal' is a girl who is pretending to be a virgin. The first line plunges us immediately into a 'dramatic' context; the speaker addresses a woman who is killing him through scorn. He pictures a time when he will be dead and she will be someone else's lover.

- Look at how the dramatic context of the poem is developed. What is the atmosphere of the bedroom scene he describes?
- How do you react to the last four lines? Do you think it is true that the poet's love is 'spent' (line 15)?
- What is the force of the word 'innocent' in the last line?

Donne's collection of poems, *Songs and Sonnets*, contains a rich variety of love poetry, of which 'The Apparition' is one example. The poems are written from many differing viewpoints and express a range of attitudes: ecstatic, confident, despairing, cynical, bitter. In so far as it seems unlikely that all the varied moods expressed through the poetry are the product of personal experience, you might be inclined to question the authenticity of these emotions. The question of *sincerity* is one which often arises when reading 'personal' poems. We must be very careful not to be sweeping in our judgments of what is 'sincere'. Donne's poems may not always be based directly upon his own immediate experience, but that does not mean to say that the feelings they express are not genuine. A poem is not like an entry in a journal; it is the product of the imagination, where all kinds of emotions can be experienced and be none the less powerful for being at one remove from direct experience. Poets often display the gift of the dramatist in bringing thoughts and feelings to life by creating and playing a part.

The next poem, by Elizabeth Jennings, takes us back into the world of direct experience.

My Grandmother

She kept an antique shop – or it kept her.
Among Apostle spoons and Bristol glass,
The faded silks, the heavy furniture,
She watched her own reflection in the brass
5   Salvers and silver bowls, as if to prove
Polish was all, there was no need of love.

And I remember how I once refused
To go out with her, since I was afraid.
It was perhaps a wish not to be used
10   Like antique objects. Though she never said
That she was hurt, I still could feel the guilt
Of that refusal, guessing how she felt.

Later, too frail to keep a shop, she put
All her best things in one long narrow room.
15   The place smelt old, of things too long kept shut,
The smell of absences where shadows come
That can't be polished. There was nothing then
To give her own reflection back again.

And when she died I felt no grief at all,
20   Only the guilt of what I once refused.
I walked into her room among the tall
Sideboards and cupboards – things she never used
But needed: and no finger-marks were there,
Only the new dust falling through the air.

Elizabeth Jennings

- How does the poet bring out her feelings towards her grandmother, both past and present?
- 'She kept an antique shop – or it kept her.' How is this idea developed in the poem?

- How would you explain the metaphor 'The smell of absences where shadows come/ That can't be polished' (lines 16–17)?
- Comment on the form and technique of this poem.

The next poem, by William Wordsworth, is also in the form of a reminiscence. It is one of a series of so-called 'Lucy poems'. The identity of Lucy has been much argued about but never resolved; in fact, it is possible that she never even existed. Would that make any difference to your response to the poem?

She dwelt among the untrodden ways

She dwelt among the untrodden ways
    Beside the springs of Dove,
A Maid whom there were none to
    praise
    And very few to love:

5 A violet by a mossy stone
    Half hidden from the eye!
Fair as a star, when only one
    Is shining in the sky.

She lived unknown, and few could know
10   When Lucy ceased to be;
But she is in her grave, and oh,
    The difference to me!

William Wordsworth

- Write a critical appreciation of this poem. How does Wordsworth bring out personal feelings here?

The next two poems have similar starting points. In both, the speaker stands by the seashore and recalls someone dear to him, now dead. Hardy's poem 'Beeny Cliff' is firmly rooted in his experience. In March 1870 Hardy visited Beeny Cliff, in Cornwall, with the woman who was soon to be his wife, Emma Gifford. In March 1913, shortly after her death, he revisited the site and wrote this poem.

Beeny Cliff
March 1870 – March 1913

I

O the opal and the sapphire of that wandering
    western sea,
And the woman riding high above with bright hair
    flapping free –
The woman whom I loved so, and who loyally
    loved me.

II

The pale mews plained below us, and the waves
    seemed far away
5 In a nether sky, engrossed in saying their ceaseless
    babbling say,
As we laughed light-heartedly aloft on that clear-
    sunned March day.

III

A little cloud then cloaked us, and there flew an
    irised rain,
And the Atlantic dyed its levels with a dull
    misfeatured stain,
And then the sun burst out again, and purples
    prinked the main.

IV

10 – Still in all its chasmal beauty bulks old Beeny to
the sky,
And shall she and I not go there once again now
March is nigh,
And the sweet things said in that March say anew
there by and by?

V

What if still in chasmal beauty looms that wild
weird western shore,
The woman now is – elsewhere – whom the
ambling pony bore,
15 And nor knows nor cares for Beeny, and will
laugh there nevermore.

Thomas Hardy

- In an appreciation of this poem, consider Hardy's power of
re-creating scenes from the past and the emotions that went
with them?
- What do the metre and rhyme scheme add to the poem?

Tennyson's poem also reflects a sense of loss. At university in
Cambridge he formed a strong friendship with a fellow under-
graduate, Arthur Hallam, who later died abroad. One of
Tennyson's finest works, 'In Memoriam', was dedicated to
him.

Break, break, break

Break, break, break,
   On thy cold grey stones, O Sea!
And I would that my tongue could utter
   The thoughts that arise in me.

5   O well for the fisherman's boy,
   That he shouts with his sister at play!
O well for the sailor lad,
   That he sings in his boat on the bay!

And the stately ships go on
10   To their haven under the hill;
But O for the touch of a vanish'd hand,
   And the sound of a voice that is still!

Break, break, break,
   At the foot of thy crags, O Sea!
15   But the tender grace of a day that is dead
   Will never come back to me.

Alfred, Lord Tennyson

- Tennyson has often been praised for his mastery of sound and metre. Do you find evidence of it here?
- How does his poem compare with Hardy's in its treatment of a similar theme?

The last three poems in this chapter have in common that they are all three addressed from men to women. The three women are very different, however, in that the first is definitely imaginary, the second possibly imaginary and the third an unknown corpse.

The subject of Alexander Pope's 'Elegy to the Memory of an Unfortunate Lady' had supposedly killed herself whilst abroad as a result of an unfulfilled passion. The poem is too substantial to print in full, but the concluding lines will give you a taste of it.

Elegy to the Memory of an Unfortunate Lady

(concluding lines)

What can atone (Oh ever-injured shade!)
Thy fate unpitied, and thy rites unpaid?
No friend's complaint, no kind domestic tear
Pleased thy pale ghost, or graced thy mournful bier.
5 By foreign hands thy dying eyes were closed,
By foreign hands thy decent limbs composed,
By foreign hands thy humble grave adorned,
By strangers honoured, and by strangers mourned!
What though no friends in sable weeds appear,
10 Grieve for an hour, perhaps then mourn a year,
And bear about the mockery of woe
To midnight dances, and the public show?
What though no weeping Loves thy ashes grace,
Nor polished marble emulate thy face?
15 What though no sacred earth allow thee room
Nor hallowed dirge be muttered o'er thy tomb?
Yet shall thy grave with rising flowers be dressed,
And the green turf lie lightly on thy breast:
There shall the morn her earliest tears bestow,
20 There the first roses of the year shall blow;
While angels with their silver wings o'ershade
The ground, now sacred by thy relics made.
So peaceful rests, without a stone, a name,
What once had beauty, titles, wealth, and fame.
25 How loved, how honoured once, avails thee not,
To whom related, or by whom begot;
A heap of dust alone remains of thee:
'Tis all thou art, and all the proud shall be!

Poets themselves must fall, like those they sung;
30　Deaf the praised ear, and mute the tuneful tongue.
Even he, whose soul now melts in mournful lays,
Shall shortly want the generous tear he pays;
Then from his closing eyes thy form shall part,
And the last pang shall tear thee from his heart;
35　Life's idle business at one gasp be o'er,
The Muse forgot, and thou beloved no more!

Alexander Pope

This poem is rather different in style from most of the others
in this chapter. It uses a great deal of poetic diction (see page
19). Black clothes become 'sable weeds' (line 9), for example.
Once again it is a poem where you need to be careful about
the question of sincerity. Pope writes in a very studied, exact
way; no word or phrase seem out of place. That does not
mean, however, that the poem is a mental exercise without
feeling; there is nothing wrong with artistry!

Two stylistic points: notice Pope's use of the rhyming
couplet here and of *end-stopping*. An end-stopped line of poetry
is one where there is a punctuation mark such as a full stop
or semicolon at the end of it. The reader has to break off as
the line comes to a conclusion. For example:

A heap of dust alone remains of thee:
'Tis all thou art, and all the proud shall be!
(lines 27–28)

Both these lines are end-stopped. By slowing the reader down
and making him pause, Pope helps to create the sense of
finality that his words convey. Generally, however, rhyming
couplets are end-stopped on the second rhyme only. The
opposite of end-stopping is known as *enjambement*. When this
device is being used, lines flow into each other either without
stopping or with only the slight pause provided by a comma.
Take, for example, these lines from Wordsworth's 'Lucy' poem
earlier in the chapter (page 78):

> She lived unknown, and few could know
>> When Lucy ceased to be;
> But she is in her grave, and oh,
>> The difference to me!

(lines 9–12)

Here enjambement and end-stopping alternate. For an example of rhyming couplets which use enjambement far more than Pope does, look forward to Browning's poem, 'My Last Duchess', in the next chapter (page 103).

- Write an appreciation of these closing lines of 'Elegy to the Memory of an Unfortunate Lady'. Look at their skilful balancing of phrases.
- How does the poem change in direction in the last eight lines?
- What is your response to this poem?

The next poem, Andrew Marvell's 'To His Coy Mistress', brings an emphatic change in mood. The poem is a powerful argument addressed to the girl who says No!

To His Coy Mistress

Had we but world enough, and time,
This coyness, Lady, were no crime.
We would sit down and think which way
To walk and pass our long love's day.
5 Thou by the Indian Ganges' side
Shouldst rubies find: I by the tide
Of Humber would complain. I would
Love you ten years before the Flood,
And you should, if you please, refuse
10 Till the conversion of the Jews.
My vegetable love should grow
Vaster than empires, and more slow;

An hundred years should go to praise
Thine eyes and on thy forehead gaze;
15 Two hundred to adore each breast;
But thirty thousand to the rest;
An age at least to every part,
And the last age should show your heart;
For, Lady, you deserve this state,
20 Nor would I love at lower rate.
  But at my back I always hear
Time's wingèd chariot hurrying near;
And yonder all before us lie
Deserts of vast eternity.
25 Thy beauty shall no more be found,
Nor, in thy marble vault, shall sound
My echoing song: then worms shall try
That long preserved virginity,
And your quaint honour turn to dust,
30 And into ashes all my lust:
The grave's a fine and private place,
But none, I think, do there embrace.
  Now therefore, while the youthful hue
Sits on thy skin like morning dew,
35 And while thy willing soul transpires
At every pore with instant fires,
Now let us sport us while we may,
And now, like amorous birds of prey,
Rather at once our time devour
40 Than languish in his slow-chapt power.
Let us roll all our strength and all
Our sweetness up into one ball,
And tear our pleasures with rough strife
Thorough the iron gates of life:
45 Thus, though we cannot make our sun
Stand still, yet we will make him run.

Andrew Marvell

In writing about this poem, you might think about some of the following questions.

- The poem is an argument. How is it developed?
- It used to be traditional in love poetry to present for praise a list of your loved one's physical features. How does Marvell handle this convention?
- What does he mean by a 'vegetable love' (line 11)?
- 'Then worms shall try/ That long preserved virginity' (lines 27–28). Consider the impact of this image.
- Look at the variety of imagery in this poem. How does Marvell use it to give force to his arguments?
- Look at his technical skills, his use of metre, sound and punctuation. How do they support the sense of the poem?

The last poem in this chapter, Seamus Heaney's 'Punishment', takes as its subject a well-preserved corpse. You may have read or seen television programmes about the bodies of primitive men and women which have been exhumed after thousands of years in a state of remarkable preservation. The peat bogs of Denmark yielded up the corpse of the girl about whom Heaney writes here. It appeared that she had been the victim of a ritual execution.

Punishment

I can feel the tug
of the halter at the nape
of her neck, the wind
on her naked front.

5   It blows her nipples
to amber beads,
it shakes the frail rigging
of her ribs.

I can see her drowned
10   body in the bog,
the weighing stone,
the floating rods and boughs.

Under which at first
she was a barked sapling
15   that is dug up
oak-bone, brain-firkin:

her shaved head
like a stubble of black corn,
her blindfold a soiled bandage,
20   her noose a ring

to store
the memories of love.
Little adulteress,
before they punished you

25   you were flaxen-haired,
undernourished, and your
tar-black face was beautiful.
My poor scapegoat,

I almost love you
30   but would have cast, I know,
the stones of silence.
I am the artful voyeur

of your brain's exposed
and darkened combs,
35   your muscles' webbing
and all your numbered bones:

I who have stood dumb
when your betraying sisters,
cauled in tar,
40 wept by the railings,

who would connive
in civilised outrage
yet understand the exact
and tribal, intimate revenge.

Seamus Heaney

- How do visual details give impact to this poem?
- How does Heaney feel towards the girl?
- How does the direction of the poem change from line 30
  onwards?
- Heaney was born in Ulster. Does that knowledge affect your
  understanding and appreciation of the poem?

6 Poems to compare

This final chapter presents a series of poems for comment and appreciation. They have been chosen in pairs so that, as well as considering them individually, you can also discuss their similarities and differences. The first pair share the same Latin title: 'Requiescat', which here means 'May she rest (in peace)'.

Requiescat

Tread lightly, she is near
    Under the snow,
Speak gently, she can hear
    The daisies grow.

5 All her bright golden hair
        Tarnished with rust,
She that was young and fair
        Fallen to dust.

Lily-like, white as snow,
10   She hardly knew
She was a woman, so
        Sweetly she grew.

Coffin-board, heavy stone,
        Lie on her breast;
15 I vex my heart alone,
        She is at rest.

Peace, peace; she cannot hear
        Lyre or sonnet;
All my life's buried here.
20   Heap earth upon it.

Oscar Wilde

Requiescat

Strew on her roses, roses,
　　And never a spray of yew!
In quiet she reposes:
　　Ah! would that I did too!

5　Her mirth the world required:
　　She bathed it in smiles of glee.
But her heart was tired, tired,
　　And now they let her be.

Her life was turning, turning,
10　　In mazes of heat and sound.
But for peace her soul was yearning,
　　And now peace laps her round.

Her cabin'd, ample spirit,
　　It flutter'd and fail'd for breath.
15　To-night it doth inherit
　　The vasty hall of death.

Matthew Arnold

In a comparison of these two poems, you might wish to
consider the following.

- Which one do you find the more convincing on a personal
  level?
- Which creates a clearer image of the dead girl?
- How do they both handle the idea of resting in peace?
- How do they compare in technique? Which seems more
  accomplished metrically?
- Which one do you find the more moving, and why?

The next two poems are paired together not so much by subject matter, although there is a sort of a link, as by their clever use of poetic form. 'Epilogue' is the concluding poem in a rather odd work which Auden wrote in the late 1920s, called *The Orators*. Yeats's poem 'An Irish Airman Foresees His Death' takes as its subject the position of Irishmen in the First World War who volunteered to fight on the British side.

Epilogue

'O where are you going?' said reader to rider,
'That valley is fatal where furnaces burn,
Yonder's the midden whose odours will madden,
That gap is the grave where the tall return.'

5 'O do you imagine', said fearer to farer,
'That dusk will delay on your path to the pass,
Your diligent looking discover the lacking
Your footsteps feel from granite to grass?'

'O what was that bird', said horror to hearer,
10 'Did you see that shape in the twisted trees?
Behind you swiftly the figure comes softly,
The spot on your skin is a shocking disease?'

'Out of this house – said rider to reader
'Yours never will' – said farer to fearer
15 'They're looking for you' – said hearer to horror
As he left them there, as he left them there.

W H Auden

An Irish Airman Foresees his Death

I know that I shall meet my fate
Somewhere among the clouds above;
Those that I fight I do not hate,
Those that I guard I do not love;
5 My country is Kiltartan Cross,
My countrymen Kiltartan's poor;
No likely end could bring them loss
Or leave them happier than before.
Nor law, nor duty bade me fight,
10 Nor public men, nor cheering crowds,
A lonely impulse of delight
Drove to this tumult in the clouds;
I balanced all, brought all to mind,
The years to come seemed waste of breath,
15 A waste of breath the years behind
In balance with this life, this death.

W B Yeats

Look first at 'Epilogue'. All poems benefit from being read out loud, but it would be particularly helpful to do so here.

- Discuss the tone of this poem, or rather its variety of tone.
- What contrasting attitudes are stressed?
- Look carefully at the shape and pattern of the poem. Why does Auden write it in this particular way?

Now consider Yeats's poem, again a good one to read aloud.

- Comment on the persona Yeats uses here. What strikes you about this airman's attitude to war and death? Why is he fighting if he neither loves his own side nor hates his enemies?

- What is distinctive about the style and shape of this poem?
- Are there any links between the viewpoints of these two poems?

The connection between the next pair of poems is certainly more obvious. Both are recollections of the experience, whilst at school, of learning of a death in the family.

The Lesson

'Your father's gone,' my bald headmaster said.
His shiny dome and brown tobacco jar
Splintered at once in tears. It wasn't grief.
I cried for knowledge which was bitterer
5   Than any grief. For there and then I knew
That grief has uses – that a father dead
Could bind the bully's fist a week or two;
And then I cried for shame, then for relief.

I was a month past ten when I learnt this:
10   I still remember how the noise was stilled
In school-assembly when my grief came in.
Some goldfish in a bowl quietly sculled
Around their shining prison on its shelf.
They were indifferent. All the other eyes
15   Were turned towards me. Somewhere in myself
Pride like a goldfish flashed a sudden fin.

Edward Lucie-Smith

Mid-Term Break

I sat all morning in the college sick bay
Counting bells knelling classes to a close.
At two o'clock our neighbours drove me home.

In the porch I met my father crying –
5 He had always taken funerals in his stride –
And Big Jim Evans saying it was a hard blow.

The baby cooed and laughed and rocked the pram
When I came in, and I was embarrassed
By old men standing up to shake my hand

10 And tell me they were 'sorry for my trouble',
Whispers informed strangers I was the eldest,
Away at school, as my mother held my hand

In hers and coughed out angry tearless sighs.
At ten o'clock the ambulance arrived
15 With the corpse, stanched and bandaged by the nurses.

Next morning I went up into the room. Snowdrops
And candles soothed the bedside; I saw him
For the first time in six weeks. Paler now,

Wearing a poppy bruise on his left temple,
20 He lay in the four foot box as in his cot.
No gaudy scars, the bumper knocked him clear.

A four foot box, a foot for every year.

Seamus Heaney

- In 'The Lesson', the child's reaction to the news of his father's death is by no means a simple one. How does the poet bring out the varied emotions he experienced?
- How does he use the image of the goldfish in the second stanza of the poem?

- In 'Mid-Term Break' what is the effect of the description of the dead boy?
- How do you respond to the last line of the poem?
- In comparing the two poems, think about the differences in the way they are set out, as well as in how the child's experience of death is presented.

The next pair of poems could possibly have appeared in Chapter 4; they both involve talking birds. However, neither could really be said to be about the subject of bird life.

The Twa Corbies

As I was walking all alane
I heard twa corbies making a mane;
The tane unto the t'other say,
'Where sall we gang and dine to-day?

5 '— In behint you auld fail dyke,
I wot there lies a new-slain Knight;
And naebody kens that he lies there,
But his hawk, his hound, and lady fair.

'His hound is to the hunting gane,
10 His hawk to fetch the wild-fowl hame,
His lady's ta'en another mate,
So we may make our dinner sweet.

'Ye'll sit on his white hause-bane,
And I'll pick out his bonny blue een:
15 Wi'ae lock o'his gowden hair
We'll theek our nest when it grows bare.

'Mony a one for him makes mane,
But nane sall ken where he is gane;
O'er his white banes, when they are bare,
20 The wind sall blaw for evermair.'

The poem is anonymous, Scottish and has a folk-tale quality about it. 'Corbies' are carrion birds, ravens or perhaps crows. Obviously for most readers there will be other initial difficulties of meaning here. It is not immediately obvious, for instance, that 'hause-bane' (line 13) means neck-bone. Some recourse to the dictionary may be needed, although many of the slightly unfamiliar words are just variations of spelling – 'hame' for 'home', for example – and can be worked out from their context.

- Once you are clear what it means, look at the way the poem tells its story of the fallen knght. What aspects of it are stressed?
- How do the 'twa corbies' view humanity?
- In what tone do they speak?
- Look at the last stanza of the poem. What point is being made?

This traditional idea of a dialogue between the two birds is given a new twist by W H Auden in his poem 'The Willow Wren and the Stare'. He takes it out of the setting of chivalry and feats of arms, and introduces instead a pair of human lovers. The dialogue of birds in the previous poem has shrunk down here to a two-line exchange at the end of each stanza. There are two other voices here: that of the narrator and that of the lover.

The Willow-Wren and the Stare

A starling and a willow-wren
    On a may-tree by a weir
Saw them meet and heard him say;
    'Dearest of my dear,

5   More lively than these waters chortling
      As they leap the dam,
My sweetest duck, my precious goose,
      My white lascivious lamb.'
With a smile she listened to him,
10   Talking to her there:
What does he want? said the willow-wren;
      Much too much, said the stare.

'Forgive these loves who dwell in me,
      These brats of greed and fear,
15   The honking bottom-pinching clown,
      The snivelling sonneteer,
That so, between us, even these,
      Who till the grave are mine,
For all they fall so short of may,
20   Dear heart, be still a sign.'
With a smile she closed her eyes,
      Silent she lay there:
Does he mean what he says? said the willow-wren;
      Some of it, said the stare.

25   'Hark! Wild Robin winds his horn
      And, as his notes require,
Now our laughter-loving spirits
      Must in awe retire
And let their kinder partners,
30   Speechless with desire,
Go in their holy selfishness,
      Unfunny to the fire.'
Smiling, silently she threw
      Her arms about him there:
35   *Is it only that?* said the willow-wren;
      It's that as well, said the stare.

Waking in her arms he cried,
  Utterly content;
'I have heard the high good noises,
40   Promoted for an instant,
Stood upon the shining outskirts
  Of that Joy I thank
For you, my dog and every goody.'
  There on the grass bank
45 She laughed, he laughed, they laughed together,
  Then they ate and drank:
Did he know what he meant? said the willow-wren –
  God only knows, said the stare.

W H Auden

- How does the narrator fulfil his role?
- Discuss the language of the lover. How would you characterise it?
- His partner never speaks. How do we view her?
- Look at the commentary provided by the two birds. How do they differ in their roles?
- Does the last line have any particular significance?
- How would you describe the poet's attitude to love in this poem?
- How serious is he?
- These poems use the same starting point to very different effect. Which do you prefer, and why?

The next two poems illustrate clearly how a similar stimulus can produce very different poems. Both poets reflect upon their growing old. Thomas Hardy looks in the mirror; W B Yeats, an Irish senator at the time of the poem, pays an official visit to a school.

I look into my glass

I look into my glass,
And view my wasting skin,
And say, 'Would God it came to pass
My heart had shrunk as thin!'

5   For then, I, undistrest
By hearts grown cold to me,
Could lonely wait my endless rest
With equanimity.

But Time, to make me grieve,
10   Part steals, lets part abide;
And shakes this fragile frame at eve
With throbbings of noontide.

Thomas Hardy

Among School Children

I

I walk through the long schoolroom questioning;
A kind old nun in a white hood replies;
The children learn to cipher and to sing,
To study reading-books and histories,
5   To cut and sew, be neat in everything
In the best modern way – the children's eyes
In momentary wonder stare upon
A sixty-year-old smiling public man.

II

I dream of a Ledaean body, bent
10   Above a sinking fire, a tale that she

Told of a harsh reproof, or trivial event
That changed some childish day to tragedy –
Told, and it seemed that our two natures blent
Into a sphere from youthful sympathy,
15 Or else, to alter Plato's parable,
Into the yolk and white of the one shell.

III

And thinking of that fit of grief or rage
I look upon one child or t'other there
And wonder if she stood so at that age –
20 For even daughters of the swan can share
Something of every paddler's heritage –
And had that colour upon cheek or hair,
And thereupon my heart is driven wild:
She stands before me as a living child.

IV

25 Her present image floats into the mind –
Did Quattrocento finger fashion it
Hollow of cheek as though it drank the wind
And took a mess of shadows for its meat?
And I though never of Ledaean kind
30 Had pretty plumage once – enough of that,
Better to smile on all that smile, and show
There is a comfortable kind of old scarecrow.

V

What youthful mother, a shape upon her lap
Honey of generation had betrayed,
35 And that must sleep, shriek, struggle to escape
As recollection or the drug decide,
Would think her son, did she but see that shape
With sixty or more winters on its head,
A compensation for the pang of his birth,
40 Or the uncertainty of his setting forth?

VI

Plato thought nature but a spume that plays
Upon a ghostly paradigm of things;
Solider Aristotle played the taws
Upon the bottom of a king of kings;
45   World-famous golden-thighed Pythagoras
Fingered upon a fiddle-stick or strings
What a star sang and careless Muses heard:
Old clothes upon old sticks to scare a bird.

VII

Both nuns and mothers worship images,
50   But those the candles light are not as those
That animate a mother's reveries,
But keep a marble or a bronze repose.
An yet they too break hearts – O Presences
That passion, piety or affection knows,
55   And that all heavenly glory symbolise –
O self-born mockers of man's enterprise;

VIII

Labour is blossoming or dancing where
The body is not bruised to pleasure soul,
Nor beauty born out of its own despair,
60   Nor blear-eyed wisdom out of midnight oil.
O chestnut-tree, great-rooted blossomer,
Are you the leaf, the blossom or the bole?
O body swayed to music, O brightening glance,
How can we know the dancer from the dance?

W B Yeats

The difference in scale is striking here. Hardy essentially makes one simple point, whereas Yeats's poem is wide-ranging and far from simple. Some parts of it are very difficult indeed. Do not be put off by the feeling that there is much you are uncertain about. Scholars who have devoted much of their academic lives to the study of modern poetry would confess that there are times when they feel that they have understood the overall pattern of a particular poem without necessarily being completely confident about its details. This comforting thought may well come in handy when you encounter the last poem in this chapter.

- Look first at Hardy's poem. How does he convey the sense of growing old here? Why does he feel bitter about 'Time'?
- What links are there between the experience described in this poem and that expressed by Yeats?

In a poem so rich in its thought as 'Among School Children' there are many topics which you could consider in writing about it. Before you do, it might be helpful to have one background detail. One of the most powerful influences upon Yeats's life was a young and ultimately unfulfilled passion for Maud Gonne, a beautiful Irish revolutionary. Hers is the 'Ledaean body' dreamt of in stanza II. (Leda was the mother of Helen of Troy.)

- Look, for example, at the way memory works in this poem.
- Consider how Yeats presents himself as a figure in the poem.
- What are the 'images' he refers to in stanza VII?
- Look at the ending of the poem. Again you may find parts difficult to understand. Listen to the music of the lines. What final impression do they leave you with?

The last two poems in this chapter differ greatly in subject matter, but both use the technique of a persona. Both leave the reader to find out more about the speaker as the poem develops. We will look first at a monologue by Robert Browning, 'My Last Duchess'.

My Last Duchess
Ferrara

That's my last Duchess painted on the wall,
Looking as if she were alive. I call
That piece a wonder, now: Frà Pandolf's hands
Worked busily a day, and there she stands.
5 Will't please you sit and look at her? I said
'Frà Pandolf' by design, for never read
Strangers like you that pictured countenance,
The depth and passion of its earnest glance,
But to myself they turned (since none puts by
10 The curtain I have drawn for you, but I)
And seemed as they would ask me, if they durst,
How such a glance came there; so, not the first
Are you to turn and ask thus. Sir, 't was not
Her husband's presence only, called that spot
15 Of joy into the Duchess' cheek: perhaps
Frà Pandolf chanced to say 'Her mantle laps
Over my lady's wrist too much,' or 'Paint
Must never hope to reproduce the faint
Half-flush that dies along her throat:' such stuff
20 Was courtesy, she thought, and cause enough
For calling up that spot of joy. She had
A heart – how shall I say? – too soon made glad,
Too easily impressed; she liked whate'er
She looked on, and her looks went everywhere.
25 Sir, 't was all one! My favour at her breast,
The dropping of the daylight in the West,
The bough of cherries some officious fool
Broke in the orchard for her, the white mule
She rode with round the terrace – all and each
30 Would draw from her alike the approving
    speech,

Or blush, at least. She thanked men, – good! but
   thanked
Somehow – I know not how – as if she ranked
My gift of a nine-hundred-years-old name
With anybody's gift. Who'd stoop to blame
35 This sort of trifling? Even had you skill
In speech – (which I have not) – to make your
   will
Quite clear to such an one, and say, 'Just this
Or that in you disgusts me; here you miss,
Or there exceed the mark' – and if she let
40 Herself be lessoned so, nor plainly set
Her wits to yours, forsooth, and made excuse,
   – E'en then would be some stooping; and I
   choose
Never to stoop. Oh sir, she smiled, no doubt,
Whene'er I passed her; but who passed without
45 Much the same smile? This grew; I gave
   commands;
Then all smiles stopped together. There she
   stands
As if alive. Will't please you rise? We'll meet
The company below, then. I repeat,
The Count your master's known munificence
50 Is ample warrant that no just pretence
Of mine for dowry will be disallowed;
Though his fair daughter's self, as I avowed
At starting, is my object. Nay, we'll go
Together down, sir. Notice Neptune, though,
55 Taming a sea-horse, thought a rarity.
Which Claus of Innsbruck cast in bronze for me!

                                   Robert Browning

Lovers of the cryptic crossword or the detective novel will
probably respond particularly well to this poem. This form of

poetry, known as the *dramatic monologue*, was one in which Browning wrote frequently; poems such as 'Fra Lippo Lippi' or 'Andrea del Sarto' are more substantial examples. The poem is a monologue, of course, because only one voice speaks throughout. The dramatic element comes from the way Browning creates a character as a speaker, places him in a particular situation and allows both to reveal themselves gradually to his readers. Since he intended them to be obliged to put in some effort before the poem could be understood and enjoyed, you are on your own!

- Look through the poem carefully and note how the speaker gradually reveals who he is, where he is, and what events in the past have combined to bring him to his present position.
- What kind of man does the speaker prove himself to be?
- What would you imagine would be his listener's reaction to what he heard?
- The last three lines stress that the speaker is an avid art collector. What is the significance of this point?
- How does Browning convey the impression of a speaking voice here?

The last poem in this chapter is the work of one of the most celebrated of twentieth-century poets, T S Eliot. It is quite a long poem and quite a demanding one, although not, I suspect, likely to prove as difficult as 'Among School Children'.

The Italian Epigraph at the start of the poem means: 'If I thought that my reply would be to someone who would ever return to earth, this flame would remain without further movement; but as no one has ever returned alive from this gulf, if what I hear is true, I can answer you without fear of infamy.'

In his poem 'The Inferno', the Italian poet Dante visits the underworld. In the depths of Hell, he encounters one Count Guido de Montefeltrano, who has been condemned to dwell within a prison formed of a single flame as punishment for giving treacherous counsel whilst on earth. When he speaks from the flame, he causes the tip to tremble. Guido points out that the only reason he is prepared to answer Dante's questions is that he believes the answers will never be reported on earth, because Dante will never be allowed to return there.

As you read it, discuss it and write about it. You may wish to consider some of the following questions.

- Who is the speaker of this poem? Can you write about him as a 'character' in the same way as you could write about the speaker in 'My Last Duchess'?
- The poem opens, 'Let us go then, you and I'. Does 'you' refer to you the reader, or to someone else?
- Where does the journey mentioned in the first line lead to?
- How do you respond to the image of the evening in lines 2–3?
- What might be the 'overwhelming question' evaded in line 10?
- How does Eliot use personification in lines 15–22?
- Who could the women be who are mentioned in lines 13–14 and 35–36?
- 'Do I dare?' (line 38). Dare do what?
- 'I have measured out my life with coffee spoons' (line 51). What does this much-quoted line suggest to you?
- 'In short, I was afraid' (line 86). Of what?
- What is the point of the reference to Lazarus in line 94?
- What is significant about the section which begins 'No! I am not Prince Hamlet' (lines 111–19)?
- 'I grow old' (line 120). How important is this idea in the poem?
- How does Eliot use the image of the mermaids in the last few lines of the poem?
- Why does 'I' become 'we' in line 129?

The Love Song of J. Alfred Prufrock

S'io credessi che mia risposta fosse
a persona che mai tornasse al mondo,
questa fiamma staria senza più scosse.
Ma per ciò che giammai di questo fondo
non tornò vivo alcun, s'i'odo il vero,
senza tema d'infamia ti rispondo.

Let us go then, you and I,
When the evening is spread out against the sky
Like a patient etherised upon a table;
Let us go, through certain half-deserted streets,
5 The muttering retreats
Of restless nights in one-night cheap hotels
And sawdust restaurants with oyster-shells:
Streets that follow like a tedious argument
Of insidious intent
10 To lead you to an overwhelming question. . .
Oh, do not ask, 'What is it?'
Let us go and make our visit.

In the room the women come and go
Talking of Michelangelo.

15 The yellow fog that rubs its back upon the
      window-panes,
The yellow smoke that rubs its muzzle on the
      window-panes,
Licked its tongue into the corners of the evening,
Lingered upon the pools that stand in drains,
Let fall upon its back the soot that falls from
      chimneys,
20 Slipped by the terrace, made a sudden leap,
And seeing that it was a soft October night,
Curled once about the house, and fell asleep.

And indeed there will be time
For the yellow smoke that slides along the street
25 Rubbing its back upon the window-panes;
There will be time, there will be time
To prepare a face to meet the faces that you meet;
There will be time to murder and create,
And time for all the works and days of hands
30 That lift and drop a question on your plate;
Time for you and time for me,
And time yet for a hundred indecisions,
And for a hundred visions and revisions,
Before the taking of a toast and tea.

35   In the room the women come and go
Talking of Michelangelo.

    And indeed there will be time
To wonder, 'Do I dare?' and, 'Do I dare?'
Time to turn back and descend the stair,
40 With a bald spot in the middle of my hair –
(They will say: 'How his hair is growing thin!')
My morning coat, my collar mounting firmly to
    the chin,
My necktie rich and modest, but asserted by a
    simple pin –
(They will say: 'But how his arms and legs are thin!')
45 Do I dare
Disturb the universe?
In a minute there is time
For decisions and revisions which a minute will
    reverse.

    For I have known them all already, known them
    all –
50 Have known the evenings, mornings, afternoons,
I have measured out my life with coffee spoons;

I know the voices dying with a dying fall
Beneath the music from a farther room,
   So how should I presume?

55   And I have known the eyes already, known
       them all —
The eyes that fix you in a formulated phrase,
And when I am formulated, sprawling on a pin,
When I am pinned and wriggling on the wall,
Then how should I begin
60 To spit out all the butt-ends of my days and
     ways?
     And how should I presume?

     And I have known the arms already, known
       them all —
Arms that are braceleted and white and bare
(But in the lamplight, downed with light brown
     hair!)
65 Is it perfume from a dress
That makes me so digress?
Arms that lie along a table, or wrap about a
     shawl.
     And should I then presume?
     And how should I begin?

          .   .   .

70   Shall I say, I have gone at dusk through narrow
       streets
And watched the smoke that rises from the pipes
Of lonely men in shirt-sleeves, leaning out of
     windows?. . .

I should have been a pair of ragged claws
Scuttling across the floors of silent seas.

     .   .   .   .   .

75   And the afternoon, the evening, sleeps so
         peacefully!
    Smoothed by long fingers,
    Asleep . . . tired . . . or it malingers,
    Stretched on the floor, here beside you and me.
    Should I, after tea and cakes and ices,
80   Have the strength to force the moment to its
         crisis?
    But though I have wept and fasted, wept and
         prayed,
    Though I have seen my head (grown slightly bald)
         brought in upon a platter,
    I am no prophet – and here's no great matter;
    I have seen the moment of my greatness flicker,
85   And I have seen the eternal Footman hold my
         coat, and snicker,
    And in short, I was afraid.

    And would it have been worth it, after all,
    After the cups, the marmalade, the tea,
    Among the porcelain, among some talk of you and
         me,
90   Would it have been worth while,
    To have bitten off the matter with a smile,
    To have squeezed the universe into a ball
    To roll it towards some overwhelming question,
    To say: 'I am Lazarus, come from the dead,
95   Come back to tell you all, I shall tell you all' –
    If one, settling a pillow by her head,
       Should say: 'That is not what I meant at all.
       That is not it, at all.'

And would it have been worth it, after all,
100 Would it have been worth while,
    After the sunsets and the dooryards and the
        sprinkled streets,
    After the novels, after the teacups, after the skirts
        that trail along the floor –
And this, and so much more? –
It is impossible to say just what I mean!
105 But as if a magic lantern threw the nerves in
        patterns on a screen:
Would it have been worth while
If one, settling a pillow or throwing off a shawl,
And turning toward the window, should say:
    'That is not it at all,
110   That is not what I meant, at all.'

No! I am not Prince Hamlet, nor was meant to
    be;
Am an attendant lord, one that will do
To swell a progress, start a scene or two,
Advise the prince; no doubt, an easy tool,
115 Deferential, glad to be of use,
Politic, cautious, and meticulous;
Full of high sentence, but a bit obtuse;
At times, indeed, almost ridiculous –
Almost, at times, the Fool.

120 I grow old ... I grow old ...
I shall wear the bottoms of my trousers rolled.

Shall I part my hair behind? Do I dare to eat a
    peach?
I shall wear white flannel trousers, and walk upon
    the beach.
I have heard the mermaids singing, each to each.

125 I do not think that they will sing to me.

I have seen them riding seaward on the waves
Combing the white hair of the waves blown back
When the wind blows the water white and black.

We have lingered in the chambers of the sea
130 By sea-girls wreathed with seaweed red and brown
Till human voices wake us, and we drown.

T S Eliot

Chronological table of poets

Sir Philip Sidney	1554–1586
Michael Drayton	1563–1631
William Shakespeare	1565–1616
John Donne	1572–1631
Andrew Marvell	1621–1678
Alexander Pope	1688–1744
William Wordsworth	1770–1850
Percy Bysshe Shelley	1792–1822
John Keats	1795–1821
Elizabeth Barrett Browning	1806–1861
Alfred, Lord Tennyson	1809–1892
Robert Browning	1812–1881
Matthew Arnold	1822–1888
Christina Rossetti	1830–1894
Thomas Hardy	1840–1928
Gerard Manley Hopkins	1844–1889
Oscar Wilde	1854–1900
A E Housman	1859–1936
W B Yeats	1865–1939
Robert Frost	1874–1963
Edward Thomas	1878–1917
T E Hulme	1883–1917
William Carlos Williams	1883–1963
D H Lawrence	1885–1930
T S Eliot	1888–1965
Hugh MacDiarmid	1892–1978
Wilfred Owen	1893–1918
Stevie Smith	1902–1971
W H Auden	1907–1973
Louis MacNeice	1907–1963
Norman MacCaig	1910–
Philip Larkin	1922–1986
Patricia Beer	1924–
Elizabeth Jennings	1926–
Thom Gunn	1929–
Peter Porter	1929–
Ted Hughes	1930–

CHRONOLOGICAL TABLE OF POETS

Index of topics

Acknowledgements

We are grateful to the following copyright holders for permission to reproduce poems:

Jonathan Cape Ltd on behalf of the Estate of Robert Graves for 'Out, Out-' from *The poetry of Robert Frost* ed. Edward Connery Lathem; Century Hutchinson Ltd for 'After Death' by Patricia Beer from *Selected Poems*; Chatto & Windus Ltd for 'Interruption to a Journey' by Norman MacCaig from *Collected Poems*; Faber & Faber Ltd for 'Musée des Beaux Arts', 'The Willow Wren and the Stare' by W. H. Auden from *Collected Poems*, 'Oh Where are you Going?' ('Epilogue') 'A Shilling Life' by W. H. Auden from *The English Auden: Poems, Essays and Dramatic Writings 1927–1939*, 'The Love Song of Alfred J. Prufrock' by T. S. Eliot from *Collected Poems 1909–1962*, 'Considering the Snail' by Thom Gunn from *My Sad Captains*, (a) 'Punishment', (b) 'Mid Term Break' by Seamus Heaney from (a) *North*, (b) *Death of a Naturalist*, 'An Otter', 'Hawk Roosting' by Ted Hughes from *Lupercal*, 'Ambulances', 'As Bad as a Mile' by Philip Larkin from *Whitsun Weddings*, 'The Explosion', 'The Building' by Philip Larkin from *High Windows*, and 'The Wiper' by Louis MacNeice from *The Collected Poems of Louis MacNeice*; authors' agents for 'My Grandmother' by Elizabeth Jennings from *Collected Poems* pub. Macmillan; authors' agents for 'The Lesson' by Edward Lucie-Smith, copyright © 1961 by Edward Lucie-Smith; Martin Brian & O'Keeffe Ltd and Mrs. Valda Grieve for 'Crystals Like Blood' by Hugh MacDiarmid; Oxford University Press for 'Mort aux Chats' by Peter Porter from *Collected Poems* (1983); authors' agents for 'The Arrival of the Bee Box' by Sylvia Plath from *Collected Poems*, pub. Faber & Faber London, copyright Ted Hughes 1965,81; James MacGibbon as Literary Executor of the Stevie Smith Estate for 'Not Waving, but Drowning' by Stevie Smith from *The Collected Poems of Stevie Smith* (Penguin Modern Classics); authors' agents on behalf of Michael B. Yeats and Macmillan London Ltd for 'Among School Children', 'When you are Old', 'The Wild Swans at Coole', 'An Irish Airman Foresees his Death' all by W. B. Yeats from *Collected Poems of W. B. Yeats*.

Longman Study Texts

General editor: Richard Adams

Novels and stories

Jane Austen
  Emma
  Pride and Prejudice
Charlotte Brontë
  Jane Eyre
Emily Brontë
  Wuthering Heights
Charles Dickens
  Great Expectation
  Hard Times
  Oliver Twist
George Eliot
  Silas Marner
  The Mill on the Floss
Nadine Gordimer
  July's People
Thomas Hardy
  Far from the Madding Crowd
  The Mayor of Casterbridge
  Tess of the D'Urbervilles
Aldous Huxley
  Brave New World
Robin Jenkins
  The Cone-Gatherers
D H Lawrence
  Sons and Lovers
W Somerset Maugham
  Short Stories
George Orwell
  Animal Farm
  Nineteen Eighty-Four
Alan Paton
  Cry, The Beloved Country
Paul Scott
  Staying On
Mark Twain
  The Adventures of Huckleberry Finn
H G Wells
  The History of Mr Polly
Virginia Woolf
  To the Lighthouse

Plays

Oliver Goldsmith
  She Stoops to Conquer
Ben Jonson
  Volpone
Christopher Marlowe
  Doctor Faustus
J B Priestley
  An Inspector Calls
Terence Rattigan
  The Winslow Boy
Willy Russell
  Educating Rita
Peter Shaffer
  Amadeus
  Equus
  The Royal Hunt of the Sun
William Shakespeare
  Macbeth
  The Merchant of Venice
  Romeo and Juliet
Bernard Shaw
  Androcles and the Lion
  Arms and the Man
  Caesar and Cleopatra
  The Devil's Disciple
  Major Barbara
  Pygmalion
  Saint Joan
Richard Brinsley Sheridan
  The Rivals
  The School for Scandal
John Webster
  The Duchess of Malfi
  The White Devil
Oscar Wilde
  The Importance of Being Earnest

Editor: George MacBeth
  Poetry for Today
Editor: Michael Marland
  Short Stories for Today